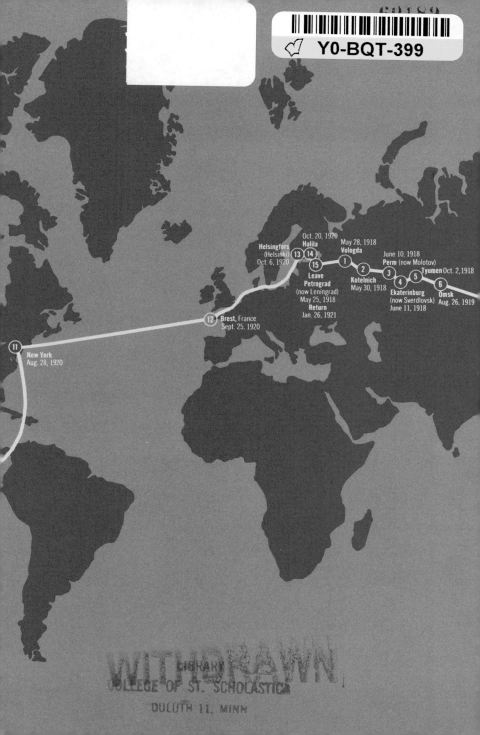

Oct. 20, 1920
Halila
Helsingfors (13) (14)
(Helsinki)
Oct. 6, 1920 (15)

May 28, 1918
Vologda
(1)

June 10, 1918
Perm (now Molotov)
(3)
(4) (5) Tyumen Oct. 2, 1918
(2)
Kotelnich
May 30, 1918
Ekaterinburg
(now Sverdlovsk)
June 11, 1918
(6)
Omsk
Aug. 26, 1919

Leave
Petrograd
(now Leningrad)
May 25, 1918
Return
Jan. 26, 1921

(12) Brest, France
Sept. 25, 1920

(11)
New York
Aug. 28, 1920

THE WILD CHILDREN

OF THE URALS

By Floyd Miller

AHDOOLO!

THE WILD

OF

WITH A FOREWORD BY

GENERAL ALFRED GRUENTHER

NEW YORK • 1965

CHILDREN
THE URALS

BY

FLOYD MILLER

E. P. DUTTON & CO., INC.

Published simultaneously in Canada by Clarke, Irwin & Company Limited, Toronto and Vancouver

Library of Congress Catalog Card Number: 65-19456

List of Illustrations

[7]

Acknowledgments

General Alfred Gruenther, while president of the American National Red Cross, suggested the writing of this book. A look into the organization's basement archives in Washington, D.C., revealed a wealth of basic documentation, some of which had been stained by flood, yellowed by forty-five intervening years. Any gaps in story material were more than compensated for by the fact that the principals involved were still alive and eager to help re-create the days and months of the strange saga of the Petrograd children.

If there was one indispensable man in that small embattled company of American Red Cross workers dropped in Siberia during the Russian Revolution, it was Riley Allen. Now retired from his longtime job as editor of the *Honolulu Star-Bulletin*, he welcomed me to the Islands and opened his own extensive files with the same generosity of spirit that has endeared him to all who have ever worked with him. Burle Bramhall, Allen's good right hand during the Siberian adventure, flew from his home in Seattle to join Allen and me in Hawaii and add his memories and his clear, unsentimental eye to the developing story.

Mother Campbell (Hannah Brain Campbell) is living out her unflagging eighties in Woodland, California. She has been on all the continents of this earth and has had enough adventures to satisfy the lustiest soldier of fortune, yet she hoots the idea of retirement. She gave me free access to her in-work autobiography and exposed me to the full impact of her robust and buoyant personality.

Mary Freeman Walker, Ward Walker's widow, lives in Maui, Hawaii, in an orchid-bedecked house close by the sea. She and John Walker, Ward's brother, were not only hospitable in the wonderful tradition of the Islands but were able to explain the detailed engineering layout of that star-crossed ship, the *Yomei Maru.*

Family scrapbooks are always a rich source of material, and Carl Myers of Minneapolis, Minnesota; Clarence Rowland of Coral Gables, Florida; and Fred Winfrey of Washington, D.C., allowed me full use of theirs. Helen Sullins, a volunteer nurse on the Siberian front, spent a day with me in St. Louis and gave me a copy of her remarkable letter which appears between these covers. Mrs. Natalia Davison, widow of Dr. Hal Davison and herself a member of the Siberian expedition, received me in Atlanta, Georgia, and contributed her husband's warmly revealing papers.

Alena Domerschikoff in Paris had vivid memories of the *Yomei Maru*'s dark and threatening voyage. Andre O'Connell in Cavaillon, France, was one of the Petrograd children and he had kept a daily diary that gave dramatic testimony to the moods of hope and despair that alternately swept the colony. Leonty Deibner, in Narbonne, France, was another of the Petrograd children and now, from his maturity, recalled and assessed the altogether remarkable trust and affection that had developed between the Russians and the Americans.

There was one vital document that eluded me for many months—the daily log of the *Yomei Maru.* It was not in the A.R.C.'s archives in Washington, nor in Riley Allen's filing cabinet, and no man could hope to remember all the details of mounting terror when nearly one thousand human beings were committed to a freighter built to accommodate only a crew of sixty. At last a copy was located in the hands of Robert Selland, nephew of Stacy Snow who had sailed the *Yomei Maru* as Riley Allen's secretary. He allowed me to have the ship's log on my desk during the entire writing of this book and my debt is obvious.

The Public Information officers of the American Red Cross brought to this project enthusiasm and excitement that had nothing to do with duty. Many a gossamer lead ended in solid fact because of the assistance of Roy Johnson, who was then Director of the Office of Public Information; Edwin Powers, Assistant Director; Mrs. Hazel Braugh, Archivist; Mabel Ward, Administrative Assistant; Clyde Buckingham; Ed Benington; and Fannie Gleeson, Director, Public Information, St. Louis Bi-State Chapter.

Foreword

The two-year odyssey of the "wild children of the Urals" is one
of the most engrossing and dramatic stories to come out of any
war. All but forgotten in the years since the First World War,
the tragedy of these Russian children during the Revolution
happened to come to my attention soon after I became president of the American Red Cross in 1957. I felt that it would
make a wonderful book.

Now the book has been written. Floyd Miller has told in
fascinating and colorful detail an epic of high adventure about
a small band of dedicated men and women and their heroic
efforts to save 800 children cut off from their parents and
homes in Petrograd and slowly starving to death in the Ural
Mountains. After two years of painstaking research and interviews with many of the surviving participants, he has marshaled the facts into a spine-tingling narrative that holds the
interest like a mystery thriller.

The files of the Red Cross are full of stories about human
courage, sacrifice and devotion, but none of them quite com-
pares with the amazing saga of the Petrograd children. Sent by
their parents to mountain camps when war danger and priva-

tion swept Petrograd in the summer of 1918, they were trapped behind the fighting lines. In the bleak winter that followed, they were reduced to begging and all were on the point of starvation when members of the American Red Cross Relief Commission to Siberia heard of their plight.

The Commission staff combed the youngsters out of the mountain wilds and began the unparalleled feat of moving them 4,000 miles across Siberia to Vladivostok. Later, when the course of the revolution imperiled their lives there, the A.R.C. Siberian Commissioner Riley Allen and a handful of other hardy souls loaded the 800 kids on a small Japanese freighter and headed east for Petrograd, 15,000 miles away.

What happened on that voyage makes up most of Floyd Miller's book. From the beginning, the obstacles to the success of the unique venture were all but insurmountable. There is nothing else like it in all the annals of the American Red Cross. The story is a cliff-hanger throughout. It's a tale of tears and hope, of sadness combined with humor, high spirits and all the music and poetry for which the Russian people are so well known. And to cap it all, Mr. Miller tells it admirably well.

Alfred M. Gruenther
Washington, D.C.
February 10, 1965

THE WILD CHILDREN

OF THE URALS

CHAPTER

ONE

Riley Allen had decided to quite his job. It was a very good job—editor of the *Honolulu Star-Bulletin*—and his friends thought him a fool to jeopardize his career at such a moment in history. This was October 1918 and World War I was in its final agonies. Peace would soon come, bringing new problems and fears. There was some talk of a depression when the arms industry shut down, of vast unemployment when the soldiers arrived home from the trenches. Oh, there were many cogent arguments against a man's giving up a job and rushing off to the far side of the world, no matter how humanitarian the project. Still, no one was really surprised at Allen's decision.

"Typical of Riley," his friends said to each other, but in tones of admiration.

The boss was not so admiring of the decision. He was Wallace R. Farrington, general business manager of the *Star-Bulletin,* a civic and political leader, and soon to be appointed Governor of the Territory of Hawaii. The tone of *his* voice held disbelief, spiked with a bit of outrage.

"You're going to quit!" he exclaimed. "I don't believe it. You just haven't thought this thing through."

"I'm afraid I have," his editor replied.

"Let me get this straight, Riley. You want to go to *Siberia* to do relief work with the Red Cross? But why?"

"I think it's essential work, sir."

"Of course, of course, but why must *you* do it? Are you unhappy here? Is this a way of asking for a raise?"

"By no means. I think the world is in a mess and I want to contribute something toward setting it straight. I didn't get in the Army. . . ."

"Because you're thirty-four years old!" Farrington exclaimed. "This is an age when you should be consolidating your career, not chucking it. Riley, do you realize that you've got one of the best spots in the whole newspaper industry? Most editors would give anything to get a job in Hawaii."

Allen grinned his agreement.

"You're a newspaperman," Farrington continued, "and you know what the Red Cross will do to you over there? Make you a press officer! You'll be pounding a typewriter, only it will be in Siberia instead of Honolulu. Now does that make sense?"

"There was some talk of that," Allen admitted, "but I hope to work into something a little more important than issuing press releases."

Farrington swung his chair around to gaze out the window at the distant curve of Waikiki Beach, fringed on one side by palm trees and on the other by long, languid waves that crested briefly, then sighed against the sand and ran back to the sea. For the moment he was unaware of the beauty before him; he was preoccupied with the problem of Riley Allen. He wished he could think of the right appeal, the right approach to the man. Part of the difficulty was that labels fit so loosely on the young editor. He was the kind of Republican that no Democrat would find reactionary; the kind of Protestant whom the Catholics knew could not think ill of their church. He was soft-spoken and completely without rancor. He had great energy but it was not tied to personal ambition and therefore did not whipsaw the sensibilities of his associates. He exuded a quizzical sort of goodwill toward all men. He was slightly built, with a round, boyish face which seemed to assume its expression of gravity only at the cost of constant struggle. He looked like a cherub unaccountably caught with a pixy's sense of humor. He listened well, and could make difficult decisions without fanfare. He attracted strong personal loyalties and no small part of the success of the newspaper had been due to the respect and affection in which the city of Honolulu held him. All these facts ran through Farrington's mind, but none of them helped him with the problem.

At last he sighed and swung his chair away from the beach scene and back to Allen. "Riley," he said, "all hell is going to break loose in Siberia. It's now under the control of the White Russians and by sending their own troops in there the Allies think they can bolster the regime and prevent the Reds from taking over. I'm not so sure. But in any event, there's going to be shooting before this is finished. I know you see this as an opportunity to help people, to feed the starving and nurse the sick, but in the process you might damn well get shot. Have you considered that?"

"Yes, sir," Allen said.

"And you still want to go?"

"Yes, sir."

"You're a stubborn man," Farrington said, letting his two hands fall heavily on the desk in a gesture of surrender. "I suppose you expect me to keep your job for you until you're ready to come home."

"No, sir. I couldn't expect that."

"Well, I'm doing it!" Farrington snapped.

On the morning of November 18, 1918, the Japanese ship *Shinyo Maru* was getting up steam for a noon sailing. The Armistice had been declared on November 11, which made the peace exactly one week old. The *Shinyo Maru* was berthed near Pearl Harbor, which, twenty-three years and nineteen days later, would receive a fierce bombing from the Japanese.

But on this particular day there was sunshine and happy excitement as the passengers gathered. Among them were twenty Red Cross volunteers from the Hawaiian Islands: doctors, nurses, sanitary engineers, railway specialists, and newspaperman Riley Allen. They wore their brand-new Red Cross uniforms with pride and some self-consciousness.

The men's khaki-colored jackets and breeches were patterned after those of the United States Army, complete with puttees, Sam Browne belts, and high stiff collars that carried the Red Cross insignia. The men were of officer rank, Riley Allen wearing the bars of a captain. The women wore the broad, flat-crowned, flat-brimmed sailor hats fashionable to the day. A small enameled Red Cross pin was attached to the hat's grosgrain ribbon. Their skirts were ankle-length, just covering the tops of their black buttoned shoes. The more daring of them called attention to their slender waists by circling them with black patent leather belts, fully four inches wide.

High tide came at noon, and the *Shinyo Maru's* whistle gave shrill announcement of her intent. The ship's first officer grabbed the polished handle of the telegraph and moved it to "slow astern." The message flashed from bridge to engine room and a tremble went through the ship as she came alive and backed slowly from her berth. Friends and relatives waved from the shore and a native stringed band struck up the haunting melody of "Aloha." The music drifted after the ship, enfolding it like a caress, and several of the younger nurses began to weep with anticipated homesickness. The ship came ponderously about, threaded out of the Islands and set a course northwest at 302 degrees. Four thousand miles over the rim of the ocean lay Vladivostok, their bleak and bone-chilling destination.

CHAPTER

TWO

It was just after dawn of November 30 that Riley Allen, standing at the bow of the ship, first saw Vladivostok. She was blushed pink by the rising sun and looked fresh and innocent. She was neither. She was an old and congested city full of four- and five-story buildings with walls made massively of stone and brick to endure the Siberian winters. Here and there a gold onion top marked an Orthodox Church and gave the otherwise drab city a touch of mystery.

She was protected from the sea by two great encircling arms of land that enclosed one of the best natural harbors in the world, the Bay of the Golden Horn. This had been the naval base of the Czar's proud eastern fleet, but the Czar was gone and so was his fleet. It had been replaced by great flotillas of troop, munition, and supply ships from all over the world. Their national flags provided a roll call of the recently victorious Allies who were now in the process of occupying and garrisoning this city.

By the time of Allen's arrival each of the Allied Powers had established its own compound and was funneling men and materials into it. Present were the French, British, Italians,

Canadians, Rumanians, Serbians, Americans, Poles, Czechs and Japanese.

The ship dropped anchor before the Red Cross compound and the passengers began to debark by small launch. A dozen Red Cross volunteers who had preceded them from the United States by a week waved excited greetings from the shore, and this was vastly reassuring to the awed and lonely newcomers.

When Allen stepped ashore he was greeted by a man who wore eagles on his shoulders but the ARC insignia on his collar. He was the commanding officer, the commissioner of what had now been formally designated the American Red Cross Siberian Commission. He was Dr. Rudolph Bolling Teusler, an outstanding American medical missionary and, until this assignment, the superintendent of St. Luke's Hospital in Tokyo. And he was not at all what Allen had expected.

Dr. Teusler's deep humanitarian instincts were incongruously wrapped in an aloof and rather aristocratic demeanor. On his thin, ascetic face he wore a clipped moustache and a small Vandyke beard. He was immaculately groomed and Allen had the conviction that no matter what long hours he spent in his uniform, it would be impervious to wrinkles.

"Awfully good to have you here, Allen," Teusler said with a small smile. There was a touch of shyness about the smile that made the man quite engaging, and Allen regretted his too quick assessment. Teusler continued, "After you're settled in, perhaps you could stop by my office for a talk. We're all in Barracks No. 7. You'll find my office on the ground floor."

Barracks No. 7 was a huge and rather ugly structure two blocks long and three stories high. It had once been a Russian military barracks, thus accounting for its lack of grace but also for its solidity. It had walls of masonry thirty-six inches thick and the narrow windows were hung with double panes of glass so that the severe winter weather would not crack them. The rooms were warmed by a unique if primitive system of radiant heating. Coal stoves were built into the side walls and out of them ran a labyrinth of chimneys. When the stoves were stoked up and the doors shut, the chimneys heated the walls of the rooms.

As Allen entered the structure he came upon a scene of great confusion, for Korean, Russian and Chinese laborers were in the process of putting up wooden partitions. The building had originally consisted of one vast two-block-long room on each of the floors, but the remodeling was to create a variety of rooms for a variety of purposes. On the first floor were the administrative offices, a recreation hall, kitchen, and dining room. The second floor was the women's dormitory and the third floor, the men's.

When Allen arrived at the third floor he found a warren of rooms formed by halfway wooden partitions. Each small room held eight cots and footlockers and though not all of them were now occupied, they soon would be when the bulk of Red Cross workers arrived from America. He found his assigned bed, unpacked, and went immediately in search of Teusler.

Dr. Teusler's office was small and spartan, containing an oak desk, half a dozen straight chairs and a large map of Siberia. When Riley Allen entered, Teusler waved him to one of the chairs and, not being a man of small talk, came immediately to the business at hand.

"We've been in great need of a good press officer," he said. He may have sensed Allen's inward flinch for he hastily added, "Most of us can organize relief trains, distribute food and medicines, nurse the sick, but to explain what we are doing, to interpret our policy, not just to the rest of the world but to the various military commanders right here in Vladivostok is a special skill."

Allen said, "As I understand the Red Cross policy, it is to give military and civilian relief to those who need it, irrespective of nationality or politics. That can be explained in one sentence."

Teusler allowed himself a wry smile. "Not in Vladivostok. There are dark suspicions of us here. It is thought we have secret and Machiavellian plans to intervene in Russia's civil war. The Whites suspect us of aiding the Reds, and the Reds are convinced we are an arm of the American military occupation. Even General Graves, commander of the American military forces here, views us with some hostility. I'm not giving you an easy assignment, Allen."

Chastened, Allen said, "It looked somewhat simpler back in Hawaii. I can see now that I have a fair amount of homework to do before I can presume to interpret anything."

During that afternoon Teusler took Allen through the torturous train of events that had led to the presence of the Red Cross in Siberia.

In June 1918 the Japan Chapter of the American Red Cross had received a cable from Dr. Russell M. Storey, YMCA field director stationed in Siberia. The cable read: "Will Red Cross work among Czech troops? Need is serious. Czech organization is prepared to furnish full cooperation and bear expenses not usually assumed by Red Cross."

Until this cable the outside world had little awareness that large bodies of Czech troops were still within Russia. The chancellories of the major powers knew it, of course, but they were uncertain what to do about it. The Czechs and the Slovaks had been subjects of the Austro-Hungarian dual monarchy empire and when the war broke out they were drafted into the army. They were unwilling subjects of the Hapsburgs and less than eager soldiers when fighting for the greater glory of Kaiser Wilhelm. They burned with nationalism and dreamed of the day when they would be independent and govern their own lands in the heart of Europe.

When thrown by their hated Austrian commanders into the Russian battlefront, they deserted by the thousands to cross over and join the Russians. Skilled soldiers when their hearts were in the battle, they formed their own legions under first the Czar's and then Kerensky's command and turned on their former oppressors. When the Russian armies began to crumble, the Czechs retained their cohesion, their spirit, and their arms. But with the Treaty of Brest-Litovsk on March 3,

1918, the war between the new Red Russian regime and the
Central Powers ended and the Czechs were in a perilous position. They could not return to their homeland where their own
ruling classes considered them traitors and would certainly
shoot them. Since they were devoted to democracy, their position in Red Russia was almost as perilous. It was only because
of so many pressing problems that Lenin had not moved to
interne them, but certainly that action would not be long delayed. It seemed imperative that they get out of Russia, even if
they had to fight their way out.

During the winter of 1917–18 the Czechs began to come
quietly together from all over Russia. In the early summer they
attacked a thousand miles of the Trans-Siberian Railway and
took it. This gave them transport as well as guns, and they
began to fight their way east toward the Siberian port of Vladivostok on the Sea of Japan. From there they hoped the Allies
would evacuate them by sea and return them to the Western
Front where they could fight against Germany for their country's independence.

The Allies had already recognized Thomas Masaryk's proclaimed Czechoslovakian Republic, pledged themselves to the
new nation's independence in any postwar settlement, and
they could not very well ignore the Czech warriors who were
battling for the same end deep in Siberia. Conferences in
Washington, London, Paris, Rome, and Tokyo resulted in the
commitment to transport the Czechs out of Vladivostok for
redeployment on the Western Front.

This decision only raised more problems. Vladivostok and
most of central Siberia were controlled by a variety of White
Russian regimes, none of them possessing cohesion or vigor.
There was a very real possibility of the Reds cutting the
Trans-Siberian Railway and even taking Vladivostok. What
then would happen to the Czechs?

There was only one conclusion compatible with the military
and political realities; the railroad and the harbor had to be
kept out of Red hands. This meant Allied military intervention.

Japan was the most vociferous in demanding intervention, for she had dreams of an empire that included the mainland. To aid the Czechs, to make Siberia a battlefield of conflicting nationalities and ideologies would, the Japanese hoped, create a power vacuum. She would be ready to fill it.

The British were strong for intervention for the clear and unconcealed reasons of ideology. There were no ambiguities in the Foreign Office; they saw Lenin out to destroy the propertied class, not just in Russia but in the world. Even as the Kaiser was being defeated, this new enemy was rising. The British did not shrink from facing the facts.

In Washington, however, all sorts of agonizing appraisals were made and remade. President Woodrow Wilson had entered the war for many high principles, prime among them being the self-determination of peoples. On the eve of victory he did not want to violate this principle in Siberia. He did not share the British prophetic vision of Bolshevism, he rather hoped that the undeniable wrongs the Russian people had suffered at the hands of their own ruling classes could be righted without creating a permanent reservoir of class hatred and exportable revolution. But he was under considerable pressure to join the Allies in the intervention, not only from London and Paris but from within his own State Department. No one wanted Japan to move into Siberia alone, and there were indications she would do so if the Allies held off.

In the end he compromised. He joined the intervention but he hedged. In a Department of State aide-memoire, issued July 17, 1918, American policy was enunciated in a series of contradictory paragraphs. Among them:

"It is the clear and fixed judgment of the Government of the United States . . . that military intervention there would add to the present sad confusion in Russia rather than cure it, injure her rather than help her, and that it would be of no advantage in the persecution of our main design to win the war against Germany. It cannot, therefore, take part in such intervention or sanction it in principle."

And then later in the same paragraph: "Military action is admissible in Russia, as the Government of the United States sees the circumstances, only to help the Czecho-Slovaks consolidate their forces and get into successful cooperation with their Slavic kinsmen and to steady any efforts at self-government or self-defense in which the Russians themselves may be willing to accept assistance."

And in the following paragraph: "At the same time the Government of the United States wishes to say with the utmost cordiality and good will that none of the conclusions here stated is meant to wear the least color of criticism of what the other governments associated against Germany may think it wise to undertake. It wishes in no way to embarrass their choice of policy."

After carrying water on at least three shoulders, Wilson then proclaimed: ". . . it [the United States] proposes to ask all associated in this course of action to unite in assuring the people of Russia in the most public and solemn manner that none of the governments uniting in action either in Siberia or in northern Russia contemplates any interference of any kind with the political sovereignty of Russia, any intervention in her internal affairs, or any impairment of her territorial integrity. . . ."

Despite this pious and cloudy document, and General Graves' determination to observe the strictest neutrality, there *was* intervention by the rest of the Allies. Within six months the foreign troops in Siberia numbered as follows: French, 760; British, 1,600; Italian, 2,000; Canadian, 4,000; Rumanian, 4,000; Serbian, 4,000; American, 7,500; Polish, 12,000; Czech, 55,000; Japanese, 68,000.

There *was* interference with the political sovereignty of Russia. There *was* intervention in her internal affairs and impairment of her territorial integrity. And out of it all came a military debacle and a political blunder of such dimensions as to sharply influence decades of future history. Yet, caught in the pressures of the moment, there seemed no way for the Allies to turn aside.

It was into this march of great and tragic events that the Red Cross was drawn. On July 1, 1918, Dr. Teusler went to Vladivostok for a firsthand inspection of conditions. They were indeed serious.

While the main body of Czech soldiers was still deep in the interior of Siberia thousands of miles from Vladivostok, a few units had arrived, fighting as they came. The first of the Czech military trains had invaded and captured the city and turned it over to a White Russian civilian government. There were many Czech wounded and diseased in the city, with inadequate facilities to care for them. A number were being treated by the medical staff of the U.S.S. *Brooklyn*, at anchor in the harbor, but many were lying in waterfront warehouses with only the most cursory attention.

Moreover, the Czechs still to the west were strung out over thousands of miles of the Trans-Siberian Railway, living in boxcars and shacks with no medical facilities and little food. Each day more of them staggered into Vladivostok, increasing the local food and medical crisis. Epidemic disease threatened the city, making no distinction between military and civilian population, between Red and White. Teusler reported this need back to Red Cross Headquarters in Washington. Headquarters accepted the responsibility and established its Siberian Commission with Teusler in charge.

THREE

Press officer was not the role Allen had hoped to play but once given the job he went about it with energy. He tramped the streets of Vladivostok to meet the people and to interview the various military commanders. The overwhelming impression of the city was the poverty and fear. Many of the necessities of life, such as shoes and candles and eyeglasses, were simply unattainable. Food had to be brought in from the surrounding countryside and since many trains were being bombed by Red guerillas, the city lived on the edge of starvation.

Moreover, Vladivostok was in the grip of a White political terror. Men were arrested without charges ever being made, there were executions without trial, and confiscation of property at the whim of the Cossack chiefs, Grigori Semenov and Ivan Kalmykov. This unholy pair were the puppets of Japan who, by its overwhelming military superiority, was the dominant power.

On November 18, 1918, Admiral Aleksandr Vasilevich Kolchak had, with the approval of the Japanese and British, taken to himself the title "Supreme Ruler of Russia." It was hoped that he could rally all the anti-Bolshevik forces and from his base in Siberia march triumphantly westward and sweep the Reds into the Baltic. As Allen made his rounds he came to the conclusion that this would not happen. Kolchak's most effective troops were the Czechs, but General Rudolf Gaida's advance had reached the high watermark of the Urals and now gave signs of receding. The truth was that the Russian masses were not rallying to Kolchak, for they tended to see him a continuing symbol of the old oppressions they had suffered under the Czar.

Allen saw all this through his trained reporter's eyes, and Teusler came to depend more and more upon him when setting Red Cross policy. Soon Allen was made secretary to the Red Cross Commission, and then assistant commissioner, second in command of the entire program.

During the winter of 1918–19 the Red Cross operated under an enormous load of military, medical and civilian relief. Their activities were stretched over 4,000 miles from Vladivostok right to the fighting front in the Ural Mountains. They operated 18 hospitals containing 6,596 beds attended by 56 American doctors, 34 non-American doctors, 182 American Red Cross nurses, 350 Russian nurses and nurses' aides, 15 Japanese nurses and 13 Chinese nurses.

The Red Cross relief trains, loaded in Vladivostok and sent westward, totaled 33 and averaged 23 loaded cars per train. They distributed 8,000 tons of supplies. Clothing was distributed to 587,000 men, 387,000 women and 775,000 children. This clothing, plus food and medicines, was being brought to Vladivostok by 30 ships from America and 92 ships from Allied countries.

In the area of military relief, the Red Cross supplied sweaters, socks, helmets, pajamas, toilet articles, bathing suits and athletic equipment to the 8,000 men of the American Expeditionary Force, the 13,330 officers and men of the Army Engineers, warship and transport crews when in port, as well as the railway dispatchers and engineers of the Russian Railway Service Corps.

This was an enormous relief operation but it was destined to grow even larger. As the Czech casualties began to mount, the Red Cross hospitals set up near the fronts nursed them; and as Czech uniforms disintegrated, the Red Cross gave them warm clothing against the terrible Siberian winter.

Perhaps the greatest comfort the Red Cross had to offer these lost and wounded men was the scrubbed and pretty faces of the American nurses, their natural good health and unfailing good spirits. Few of them were formally trained, they were volunteers who had received a quick course as nurses' aides and were then sent into the savagery of Siberia.

A typical volunteer was Helen Sullins of St. Louis, Missouri. Both her brothers were in the Army and in 1917 she volunteered for Red Cross work. She arrived in Vladivostok with the advance nursing units in 1918 and was soon in the front lines. She wrote her family a gripping letter that revealed what an American nurse's life was like. The following letter was written on Christmas Day:

It will be difficult for you to imagine an atmosphere so filled with hate and ill-will that it almost bristles. Where soldiers of so many nations are gathered, in close quarters, in midwinter, there is little good will. Alas! Alas! Last night we were so happy, all huddled together in our cold room, popping corn, cutting into strips the only bright paper we could find in all Siberia (salvaged from our own trunks), roasting diminutive Chinese peanuts, and putting all the little trinkets we could find into Comfort Bags for the soldiers in our Hospital. Then it was so easy to forget that we are 6,000 miles from home and plenty, and that our food is cold fish and frozen black bread. Yes, that was last night.

At midnight an order came to evacuate. All our possessions, our tinned food—all—were packed into our bags and we were hurriedly huddled into ezvostics and taken under cover of darkness to the river. Here we were again hurried onto a shaky Russian river boat and transported across the river, filled with floating blocks of ice, which made me think of the runaway slaves escaping in Uncle Tom's Cabin, to the other side where our train awaited us. All we know is that we have been compelled to leave our wounded and helpless men behind in a hospital that is soon to fall into the hands of the invading Reds. Sentinels are everywhere, stray firing is heard on every side. In this medieval city the midnight stillness is also broken by racing motorcycle messengers, tearing down the narrow cobbled streets and across the cathedral square. The city is under martial law. A band of Cossacks, riding superbly, kicks up a cloud of drifted snow; church bells are ringing wildly, as they can only ring in Russia; the streets are filled with people. Excitement runs high, but why, why are we being taken away so hurriedly? Have we not seen rioting before? We are too tired, too disturbed, too discouraged to let the excitement take hold of us. We do not even think of Christmas.

It is the day before Christmas. A brilliant sunset lights up a snow-covered waste. We are on neutral territory, the American consul general's train. All day we have been "prisoners," not allowed to leave our narrow coupes; forbidden to go to the windows, even though we can hear the constant rat-tat-tat of the machine guns, but as evening draws nearer the firing is less and the day no doubt will end in peace. Night will soon be here, for we already hear the howling of Russia's hordes of stray dogs. We beg, we plead to be allowed to make one trip back to the hospital that has been the only home we have known. We cannot forget the Comfort Bags, all the little treasures we collected from our own scanty store, just to make Christmas possible for the men. We had waited so long for an opportunity to hear the gay Czechs sing their Christmas songs and perhaps, a Russian, if he be not too sick. It is Christmas Eve! We win! A guard is sent for. Into our heavy boots, hoods, valenkies we jump and soon we hear the crunch, crunch, crunch of the Russian Guards over the dry snow on their way to our train to conduct us back to the city and our Hospital! Does it matter that all Russia is at war? We have won; we are on our way to the hospital! We form into line, two abreast; on either side of us a row of tall Astrakhan-capped Russian soldiers in long tunics, carrying odd-looking rifles with long bayonets, slung across shoulders already stooped from long months of war without bread. Down the railroad yard we go,

between rows and rows of trains, past the station, across an
open space, to the old pontoon bridge, three hundred years
old. How amazingly bright the stars are, how crisp and clear
the air! We are across the river, again in the old city, again
we go through the narrow streets, this time not as one fleeing.
On we go through the Chinese and Tartar quarters, up more
narrow streets, across the cathedral square and on up the hill,
past the old monastery, and on to the hospital.

We cross the road and start to enter the gates. "Stoya!" A
sharp command halts us. It is the military guard, Red, no
doubt, halting our White guard. Is our venture going to end
in sad disappointment? Quickly one of the girls draws back
her cape, points to the Red Cross on her arm and says, "Ameri-
kansky Croana Crest. Zuda psalster?" (The American Red
Cross. May we pass?) Without another word the guard says,
"Mozna." (Forward.) We make our way to the door and our
guard goes back to the barracks to return for us within an
hour or so.

It is too good to be true! We are back in the old familiar
corridors and the huge rooms of what was once a technical
school connected with the monastery, now the only hospital
within 3000 miles. We rush through the wards, doing our best
to let the poor sick Russian soldiers know and feel that we
have come back; that we have not deserted them in the face
of danger. Too sick, too apathetic, too discouraged, they do not
respond. Someone thinks of the Comfort Bags and we race off
to get them. As we start down the corridor that leads to the
big dormitory we are again halted. This time by our old Czech
friend, with his kindly "Naznais sistra!" He cannot believe his
eyes. The "sistras" are back!

The news spreads through the hospital. Perhaps the sisters
have not gone? Perhaps, perhaps? A ray of hope seems to light
up his face. We load ourselves with the bags and this time
we go to our favorite ward—the Czech ward—where we know
that we will receive a hearty welcome. As we go up the steps
to what was once a chapel, we hear a rustling in the corridor
above. To our amazement we see lined up against each wall
a row of our old friends, the German War Prisoners, each
with a great bundle of rushes in his hands. From each side

they step forward, brush the floor before us, then make the sign of the cross over each of us as we proceed. They are back at home, carrying out an age-old custom of chasing the evil spirits away so that the spirit of Christmas may pass unmolested. Old, war-worn men, many of them past fifty, but all of them at home tonight—boys.

We rush to the door, throw it open, and as best we can, we greet the surprised men with "Naznais." Heads pop up. "Sistra! Sistra! Sistra!" comes from a dozen at once. We pass between the rows of beds, giving each a Comfort Bag, and in broken German, English and Russian, we wish them a Merry Christmas. One bright little fellow, much younger than the others, sits up in bed and begins to sing "Stille Nacht." Through tears and laughter, in German, Czech and English, we sing that old carol to the end. In the midst of our celebration a loud rap is heard and in strides an officer. He announces the arrival of the Guard. Like a flash we are back to reality. Can it be that we are in Siberia? Can it be that the whole face of Russia is changing? A minute ago all was warmth and good cheer and peace and now guards, armored trains, Siberian snows and black bread. Slowly we reach the outer door. A RED GUARD!!! A RED GUARD!! All Russia had gone Red. What of it? We shrug our shoulders—have we not had one hour of Peace on Earth, Good Will to Men? Will it be the last Christian Christmas in Russia?

FOUR

The Minister of the Interior in Kolchak's government was a round-faced and soft-spoken little man whose hapless job was to receive the battle news from the front and pass it on to the Admiral. The news was invariably bad and Kolchak's reaction invariably explosive, for the "Supreme Ruler of Russia" had a terrible temper. Admiral Kolchak, who charmed the British with his manners when seeking their support in London, who displayed impeccable politeness to the Japanese in Tokyo, was given to barracks language when dealing with subordinates. His staff went to inordinate lengths to shield him from annoyance and the Minister of the Interior withheld many small, unhappy rumors and bits of news.

When he heard that Major Riley Allen (recently promoted from captain) was waiting in the outer office to see him, he made a small inward grimace. It was certain to be trouble, everything that came across his desk was trouble. He sighed heavily and told his secretary to admit the American.

They greeted each other cordially, then the minister made a steeple of his fingers, poked them into the soft flesh of his second chin and said, "What can I do for you, sir?"

"There have been some strange rumors going about the city . . ."

"But of course," the minister smiled. "This is Vladivostok. One can hear what one wishes to hear."

"I do not wish to hear these particular stories but they persist and I am of the opinion there is some substance. It is said that near the battlefront in the Urals there are bands of wild children. They are reported to be starving, dressed in rags and traveling in packs. Several Czech officers report they have attempted to talk to them, but at the first advance they take to their heels and disappear into the woods. Apparently they have no parents but stay together with some sort of pack loyalty."

"Ah," said the minister noncommittally.

"They don't seem to be ordinary orphans of war, they don't have any roots in the area they travel. Apparently they are of all ages from toddlers to teen-agers. It's as if they had been brought into the mountains from someplace else and just dumped down and left to exist as best they can."

"Mmmmm," the minister said.

"I wondered, sir, if you had heard these stories?"

"Yes, I believe so," the minister said grudgingly.

"What do you make of it?"

"It's difficult to tell."

"You've reported this to Admiral Kolchak?"

The minister spread his hands. "The Admiral is so occupied with important things that I did not feel it right to burden him with anything so minor as . . ."

"Starving children?" Allen supplied rather sharply.

The minister ignored the tone and went on, reasonably, "We are having difficulty supplying our troops. We could not possibly undertake the care of several hundred wild children."

"What of the Russian Red Cross?"

A shrug of regret. "The Russian Red Cross has all but ceased to exist. No, Major Allen, if anything is to be done for such

children it would have to be your great and good American
Red Cross."

"I thought as much," Allen said grimly.

Later that afternoon Allen sat across the desk from Dr. Teusler and reported his conversation with the minister. Having
made up his mind that the Red Cross had an obligation to
rescue the children, he had come prepared with maps and
logistics. He spoke earnestly while his superior listened with a
sober face.

When Allen had finally completed his case, Teusler said, "I
take it there is no certainty that these bands of wild children
exist."

"No certainty but every probability," Allen replied. "I
would propose that our field directors in the Omsk area be
instructed to make a search."

Tuesler leaned over the maps spread on his desk. "The areas
where they are reported are . . ." he marked the map with a
pencil, "Tyumen, Chelyabinsk, Petropavlovsk, all on the eastern slope of the Ural Mountains. And all in the battle area."

"Yes, sir," Allen said, admitting the danger.

"We could never penetrate that deeply into Siberia without
military guards on our relief trains."

"The starving children . . ."

Teusler held up his hand to interrupt. "I quite agree with
you that we must reach those children if it is at all possible.
But, you see," he gave a wry smile, "it does bring up the
problem of General Graves."

General William S. Graves, commander of the American Expeditionary Force in Siberia, had not wanted this assignment
but had taken it under the urging of Newton D. Baker, Secretary of War. Baker foresaw that the presence of foreign troops
in Siberia would produce various degrees of hostility from the
Russians, and even damaging tensions between the Allies.
What was needed was an American commander who would

not panic, was not trigger-happy, would firmly adhere to President Wilson's aide-memoire. General Graves was such a man.

Graves considered the aide-memoire as an order to observe the strictest neutrality toward Russia's civil war, and he felt both impatience and suspicion of any man who did not share his narrow view of the sprawling document. He became particularly incensed at the Red Cross relief program. In a series of abrasive meetings with Dr. Teusler he pointed out that the war in Europe was ended and the Czech military activities were a direct intervention in Russia's internal affairs. He demanded that the Red Cross stop supporting such intervention by giving food and medicines to the Czechs.

With equal firmness Dr. Teusler announced that the Red Cross was giving succor to all, regardless of politics. The Red Cross hospitals took in any wounded soldier, whether Red or White, the relief trains fed all starving without regard to political belief. Under this long-held Red Cross tradition of nonpartisan relief, it would be both illogical and inhuman to withhold clothes and medicine from freezing soldiers wounded in a venture supported by the Allies. It was contrary to the humanitarian principles on which the Red Cross had been founded.

Graves and Teusler were not unlike in temperament. Both were economical with speech, firm of purpose, and found compromise difficult where duty was involved. And when such men saw their duties through different prisms, these very similarities set each hard against the other.

The depth of feeling was revealed when years later Graves wrote in his book *America's Siberian Adventure:*

"I thought it advisable to tell him [Czech General Gaida] not to expect American troops to go west of Lake Baikal, as he was being used by Allied representatives to do what he could to get each nation to send troops west.

"Unfortunately for unity of action, Dr. Teusler, handling the American Red Cross, came into the picture at this time, and it seemed to be very common knowledge that he was a cousin of Mrs. Woodrow Wilson. He was a very staunch Autocrat . . .

He appeared to be more in sympathy with the British, French and Japanese attitude than he was with the American policy of non-interference."

And later in the book: "As previously stated, Dr. Teusler, head of the American Red Cross, had no sympathy for the aspirations of the Russian people. I am sorry to have to record this fact, but truth demands that I state that the American Red Cross in Siberia was acting as a supply agent for Kolchak . . . I had been furnishing guards for Red Cross trains to Omsk thinking these supplies were to be delivered to the Russian people . . . This put the American troops in the position of issuing supplies to Kolchak troops, and I had to notify Dr. Teusler that if this ever happened again he would get no more guards for his trains from me."

It was into this atmosphere of mutual distrust that Riley Allen dropped the problem of the starving children. Teusler and Graves, the two implacably alike men, discussed the problem at some length and discovered, each to his own surprise, that this issue did not exasperate their relationship but tended to heal it. Graves agreed that *if* the starving children were found, and *if* the Red Cross undertook to feed, shelter and clothe them, armed military guards would be assigned the relief trains headed for the Ural Mountains.

Teusler reported the agreement back to Allen, saying, "You may instruct our field directors in the area of Omsk to be alert for these children and if possible make contact with them."

"Right away," Allen smiled, not revealing that ARC field directors were already doing exactly this.

FIVE

Tyumen was a silent and dying city. It lay just to the east of the Ural Mountains and was surrounded by the fertile Siberian plains. It had once been a thriving center of agricultural commerce, but that was before the war and the civil war, before the young men had been drafted, before the raids of terror and confiscation by both the Reds and the Whites, before the ruble had become worthless. Now, in the winter of 1918, the peasant farmers no longer came to market in Tyumen, they stayed holed up in their *isbas*, huts half of timber and half of mud, and hoarded what food they had for themselves. And so the city, wearing its cold white snow like a shroud, was starving slowly to death.

On the northern edge of town stood a rambling, three-story wooden house whose owner, one of Tyumen's leading merchants, had fled at the time of the Czar's abdication. During the first days of the Revolution the empty house had been stoned and looted by the Reds, leaving it little more than a shell. Month by month it became more ravaged, for fuel was scarce in Tyumen and people began ripping the wooden scrollwork from the eaves, the pendants and finials off the roof peaks, columns from the front and rear porches. If the place had not suddenly been reoccupied in the late fall of 1918, the house would have been cannibalized right down to its foundations.

It wasn't the owner who had returned, but a band of children. They had come quietly out of the night, stuffed rags in the broken windowpanes to keep out the winter wind, and on the following morning had descended upon the town to beg from door to door for food. There were about two hundred of them ranging in age from three to eighteen and they were accompanied by a dozen young adults.

They made a gaunt and pitiful parade through the streets. Their faces were pinched with hunger, their bodies clothed in rags, their feet protected from the snow by crudely made bark shoes. The strangest thing of all was their self-discipline. They did not whine and wheedle, they did not purposely display their wasted bodies; they asked for food with quiet dignity, and when it was given they properly thanked the donor. The citizens were most curious and demanded to know how they happened to be in Tyumen. It was a simple story the children told.

The previous spring they had come to the Urals to set up summer camp and school, planning to return home to Russia proper in the autumn. But the battle lines of the civil war had advanced on them from the east, then swept beyond to cut them off from their homes, throwing them at the mercy of the Siberian countryside.

It was a story simple enough to be true, and full of a horror that had become so commonplace in this land that, once having heard it, the citizens of Tyumen felt less responsibility for the children and gave less bread. As the winter deepened and their own hunger pangs sharpened, they gave none at all. The children turned from beggars to thieves, full of desperate cunning, and all the doors of all the houses in the town became locked against them.

Had anyone in Tyumen been observing the children closely, they would have noted that whenever a child obtained food he didn't stuff it greedily into his mouth but carried it quickly back to the old house where he lived. They all had a remarkable loyalty to each other, a sense of belonging, of kinship, and they took the food back to be shared.

This feeling of almost family love and responsibility had not developed without reason; there was in their midst a mother symbol who gave them love and received it in return. She passed out the food with complete impartiality, she mediated disputes with unquestioned justice, she told stories and sang songs to the tiny ones, she showed the face of courage to the older ones.

Her name was Maria Gorbochova and she had come with them as one of the teachers. During the happy summer months she had become a favorite of the children, for she never got impatient with them, never got out of sorts as some adults often do. The fact was that Maria was barely an adult herself, being just twenty, and she had not lived long enough to take on the habit of impatience. Her problem had been to prevent herself from giggling when the children giggled, to stop her legs from running when the children ran. She did her best to be dignified but she didn't fool the children into thinking she was distant from them. They knew she could be wonderfully silly at times.

She had that rarest of teaching gifts, a contagious curiosity. She had only to give one of her conspiratorial grins and exclaim, "Let's find out about Alexander the Great!" and her class couldn't wait to get the history books open. It always seemed to them that they were *discovering* pieces of history; they were convinced that no one had ever turned up exactly what they and Maria Gorbochova came upon. They were co-discoverers and the adventure bound them closely together. The children in her classes were possessive of Maria, they felt she belonged to them in a special way, almost as if they had secret handclasps and passwords.

Now, in the winter, things had changed. There were no giggles, no discoveries (schoolbooks had been burned for meager heat); there was the constant pain of hunger and the cold that seemed to penetrate to the very center of one's body, as if there were no flesh for protection. Yet Maria Gorbochova was the same. She didn't *look* the same, her stocky young figure had wasted to gauntness, her round and ebullient face was now thin and thoughtful. All the childishness had been wrung out of her to leave her an adult, old for her years. But she had not bent beneath this forcing; she had strengthened. The softness of love had remained, but surrounded and stiffened by a sense of responsibility.

It was Maria who thought ahead, and when the doors of Tyumen began to shut against them that December she devised a new system to obtain food. She organized the older children into small bands and sent them into the countryside in search of farmers whose hearts might be touched.

At the beginning it was the seventeen- and eighteen-year-olds who went out, but as the situation grew more desperate it became necessary to send younger and younger children. The day came when Peter and Fedor, each eleven years old, were to be added to the countryside search, and Maria took them aside for instructions.

"Ask for the food as a gift," she said, "explaining to them about the young ones we have. If they refuse, then offer to buy some food. If they again refuse, go on to the next farm. Don't steal."

She pressed into Peter's hands some rubles which they all knew to be practically valueless. Stealing was now about the only way any of them got food, but Maria refused to recognize the fact. They were living a lie, but a necessary lie. She had a final thing to say to the boys, and she said it with some difficulty. "If you find a kind family that will take you in for the winter, you had better stay with them. But please come back and let me know."

There came a sound at the rough planked door and the old man and old woman stopped eating and looked at each other in alarm. Spoonfuls of black mushroom soup remained suspended in midair as they waited for the sound to repeat. A long moment of silence seemed to promise that whatever was on the other side of the door had gone away, but then it came again, a soft knock. The old couple slowly expelled the breaths they had been holding, lowered their spoons back into the soup bowls and sat quite rigid with speculation.

It was night outside and no time for a friend to call. And if not a friend, who? This farm and this *isba* were remote from the civil war, and yet not too remote for guerillas to find and plunder. The farmer had heard stories about such visits in the middle of the night, stories he had tried to put out of his mind, but now they came flooding back to him as he sat still and listened.

He was dressed in a faded and patched tunic over rough breeches tucked into mud-encrusted boots. His blunt and heavy hands were habitually half-closed from long years of gripping hoe and rake, and his face, behind a yellowish white beard, was passive and innocent. He was a peasant, a man who worked with the earth and the seasons, and not the type normally involved in revolutionary plot and counterplot. Yet a thoughtless word, a gesture even, could be sufficient to condemn a man, and the old peasant searched the recent weeks for any indiscretion he might have committed. That he could find none did nothing to ease his alarm, and when the knock came for the third time he crossed himself, stood up and walked to the door with dragging steps.

The door opened creakingly and yellow lamplight rushed out into the night to reveal two children, boys of eleven years. They were dirty, their clothes in rags, and on their feet were shoes made of bark. They stood poised to run, but when the man made no threatening gesture, they relaxed a bit. The larger one, whose name was Peter, said, "We desire to buy some food." From his pocket he extracted a handful of rubles.

Even before the appearance of the money the farmer had judged them city boys, rich boys. Though their clothes were tattered there was a delicacy of face and limb that marked their origin. How they had gotten to his farm he could not imagine, nor did he allow himself to speculate. Knowledge could be dangerous, any kind of knowledge. It was best for a man to eat and work and sleep and know nothing. Still, these boys were at his door, and by reason of nothing he had said or done, and it would be foolish to turn good fortune away. Even with their soft skin and city muscles they could be useful. He swung the door wider and stood aside for them to enter.

It was staggeringly hot in the hut and many pungencies fought for attention. There was the fermenting odor of the earthen floor upon which many liquids had been spilled over the years, and above that rode the acridness of human sweat. Through it all came the sweet, fresh mouth-watering odor of newly baked bread. It was but a single room and crowded by the few pieces of rude furniture. A trestle table and three birch log chairs stood in the middle of the room, and on one wall was a double bed which sagged under the weight of its gray, lumpy coverings. Against the opposite wall stood the one prideful piece of furniture, a factory-made chiffonier of golden oak with drawer handles set on brass plates formed into clusters of grapes. On top of the chiffonier was a samovar.

Above the samovar, nailed to a log supporting the roof rafters, was an ikon, a slab of narrow wood about eight inches long and on which was painted Saint Nicholas. He was supposed to bring good luck and happiness to the house in which he dwelt, though the artist must have been unaware of this fact. Everything about the figure drooped in the most dispirited manner, and between bangs and beard a pair of doleful Russian eyes glanced to one side as if seeking escape from the weariness of sainthood.

On the third wall, opposite the door, was a woodburning stove and before it stood the farmer's wife. She had not survived the years as well as her husband. Toil had made him knotty and hard, but it had dried and bent the woman, made her brittle and sexless. Her face was so seamed as to have lost the capacity for expression, but when she saw the children her eyes turned gentle and remembering. She went to them at once, seated them at the table and began to feed them. There were bowls of black mushroom soup, noodles with milk, great chunks of fresh bread, and finally hot and bitter tea. As soon as they had eaten they grew sleepy and the farmer indicated they could sleep on the floor of the passageway to the door. They lay down and were immediately unconscious.

"You fed them too much!" the farmer hissed at his wife.

"They were hungry."

"They could have eaten less."

"I saw them offer you money."

"And what good is that?" he demanded angrily. "Who will take money these days?"

She shook her head, for it was a subject about which she was completely confused. Throughout her life money had been a rare and precious thing. Daydreams had been built around a handful of rubles. She had seen men cheat and lie for money. She had once seen murder done for it. Thrift, on the other hand, had been one of the moral pillars of her life. To be suddenly told that money was valueless—well, she could not have been more amazed if someone had announced, convincingly, there was no God.

Her husband had little more understanding of this strange new fact about money, but he was of enduring stock. If money was of no value, then one learned to get along without it. He said to her, gesturing toward the boys, "They can earn their food."

She glanced at the children who in sleep seemed smaller and frailer, and she made a soft, clucking sound through her toothless gums.

An hour before daylight Fedor and Peter were nudged awake by the toe of the farmer's boot. They yawned and stretched and discovered they had a new agony, for the hut was crawling with lice. It seemed that every inch of their bodies burned and itched with vicious little bites. Yet, strangely, the man and woman scratched not at all.

After a breakfast of bread and milk and tea, the farmer said, "I will sell you food if you help me bring in the wood from my field." The children did not answer at once and he took it that further explanation was necessary. "My son has gone off to fight."

Peter and Fedor agreed to the proposition and the farmer went outside to hitch a horse to a crude sleigh. They all rode in the sleigh across the snow-covered fields to a stand of birch. The children now discovered they were expected to chop the trees down and cut them into lengths. They worked slowly, their strength hardly adequate to the task, and frequently they had to return to the *isba* to warm themselves. By the time of the noon meal they were quite exhausted and it was clear to the farmer they were capable of no more heavy work this day. As he viewed the stack of wood under the shed by the *isba* he was not entirely dissatisfied, though he thought he should be. He rather begrudged them the size of the meal they consumed.

His wife had no such feelings and kept placing stacks of pancakes before the children. The more they ate the greater her pleasure, whereas the farmer counted each pancake and kept altering upward the price he would charge for the bread they wished to buy. Money was of no value, to be sure, but one never knew what the future might hold. Just as it had suddenly and unaccountably become worthless, so might it suddenly and unaccountably be again the source of man's security and comfort. It would be madness not to lay up the stuff when the opportunity was presented. He decided upon ten kopecks per loaf of bread.

Having decided that, his mind was free for other things and his curiosity grew strong. Though he knew knowledge to be dangerous, he could not help himself.

"Where did you come from?" he finally blurted out.

"Petrograd," Peter answered.

There was a moment of stunned silence in the hut. Then the old woman said, with a slow release of disbelieving breath, "Petrograd?"

The old man was even more amazed. "Petrograd," he murmured to himself, and then, looking at the boys with new respect he repeated the word with a savoring sort of sound, "Petrograd!"

Never in their whole lives had they known a person from so distant and grand a place as Petrograd. And to think that two people from Petrograd now sat with them, ate with them. True, they were children, but that did not make them the less unique. The old people were awed and a bit ill at ease.

"What is it like in Petrograd?" the old man asked.

Peter, who was the raconteur of the two, stretched lazily and said, "Well . . ."

It was clear that he would give himself airs during the telling.

SIX

Peter Azaroff's father had been the stage manager of the Theatre Michel, the Petrograd equivalent of Paris's Comédie Française, and the child had developed an actor's flair with a story. And the story he had to tell was one of the great human dramas of the century, for he and his family had lived through the Russian Revolution. True, he had seen but bits and pieces of it, but sufficient to hold his peasant audience enthralled.

Life had been good for the Azaroff family. They lived on an upper-middle-class street called the Large Mews, not far from the theater, which was on a street called the Smaller Mews. Since the theater season was only from October through December, vacations were frequent and the family spent long periods in their country *dacha* in the province of Finland. Then came World War I and the Germans overran Finland and requisitioned the *dacha,* and there were no more vacations. As the Russian armies suffered defeat after defeat, life became bleak in Petrograd. Food was scarce, there was no white bread at all and the family had to take turns standing all day in queues for a ration of fifteen grams of flour mixed with potato peelings and wood shavings.

If it was a hard life, there was also excitement, especially for
a boy. Peter soon learned that the most saleable commodity
was a newspaper and he became a newsboy. All the political
factions published journals, and he sold the Kadet paper one
day, the Menshevik the next day, the Social Democratic the
next. The warmest place to sell was on the streetcars and he
spent each day traveling endlessly through the town.

Petrograd, in the fall days of 1917, was a convulsed city. The
Czar had abdicated and the government was headed by the
moderate Kerensky, but there was no peace in the streets.
Every place Peter went he found crowds demonstrating,
speakers haranguing.

"I saw Lenin," Peter said to the farmer and his wife. He was
disappointed in their response to this momentous announcement. Lenin was little more than a name to them. Peter said,
"He was speaking in front of the palace of the Czar's mistress."

This time he succeeded in shocking the old couple and they
quickly crossed themselves.

"Great crowds listened to him," Peter continued, "but he
spoke so softly it was hard to hear him. You had to wait your
turn. After he made a speech, the people in the front would
leave and the people in back would come up close and he'd
make the speech over again. He did that all day long."

"What did he say?" the farmer asked.

"He said that people were starving and they should be fed."

The old man nodded. He could agree with that. He thought
of the countryside around him where the grain rotted in the
fields because nobody would buy it, and he shook his head in
complete confusion.

"Lenin's pants were too long for him," Peter said irrele-
vantly. Then, brightly, "One time I was walking home and a
horse fell dead in the street. Everyone ran off the sidewalks
and jumped on him and pulled him apart and hid pieces of
him under their coats. Soon there was nothing left except the
empty harness and some blood on the street. The owner didn't
get any of his own horse and he was so mad he wanted to fight

somebody. But there was nobody to fight. They'd all gone home to eat."

This was not the way the old couple had envisioned Petrograd. They had hoped to hear stories of beautiful palaces and glittering balls.

"I saw a man killed," Peter continued relentless. He had, in fact, seen many men killed, but this killing he remembered particularly.

"A man sold a loaf of bread on a street corner, and when the woman who bought it broke off a piece she found it was a stick covered over with a thin layer of dough. The people in the street chased the man and caught him and hanged him from a street lamp. He was there for almost a week and I saw him every day. He would swing when the wind blew."

Peter was not trying to shock, he was merely reporting. Children tend to be matter-of-fact, even when faced with horror. The child's real world is within himself and he observes the adult world rather distantly. There is much he sees that baffles him but not really much that surprises him.

The Russian front against the Germans collapsed in February 1918 and deserting soldiers flooded back into Petrograd, turning the food situation from critical to desperate. To save some of the younger generation from crippling malnutrition, the Russian Red Cross conceived the plan of sending as many as possible to summer camps in western Siberia where the harvest was good. Since the Bolsheviks would not appropriate any money for this project, the children had to be sought among the middle- and upper-class parents who could pay the expenses involved.

Recruitment proceeded through the winter and early spring for what came to be known as The Petrograd Children's Colony. Eight hundred children were enrolled and along with teachers and nurses began to leave for Siberia in May 1918. The Azaroffs enrolled Peter and he was assigned to the second group of children who would leave on May 25.

Packing nothing but light summer clothes, his schoolbooks

and his mandolin, Peter and his parents left their apartment that morning, took a tram to the Finnish station where they found that Military Hospital Train No. 2218 had been assigned to the Colony and would carry 420 boys and girls to Koure. This town had once been a fashionable spa and lay just beyond the Ural Mountains in the rich Siberian plain.

Peter was in car No. 20 where, to his delight, he found a school friend named Fedor Denisov. The car was under the command of a young school teacher named Nikolay Borsouk, who assured Mr. and Mrs. Azaroff that he would look after Peter, feed him up and return him in the fall. Farewells were said with no more emotion than ordinarily attends a child's departure for summer camp.

Late at night on May 25 the train of thirty cars moved out of Petrograd, went a few miles and stopped. Hours later it went another few miles and stopped. The Colony had the lowest traffic priority and had to give way constantly to food trains, or military trains, or almost anything else that ran on the cluttered tracks. On the morning of May 26 they crawled through poor and sandy land that frequently peaked into sterile dunes. They crossed the Neva River and entered upon the main Nikolayevskiy line, but progress was only slightly better. All that day and the next the children saw sidings full of rusting locomotives. There was desperate need for transport but neither the materials nor the men to repair these engines. Fedor started counting them and got to six hundred before he lost interest.

By May 29 they were no farther than Galich and they spent the entire day there because of rumors that the bridge over the Vyatka River had been blown up. By whom they didn't know. The children left the train and scattered over the countryside to buy food, but the peasants refused to sell anything except milk. The train moved on at six that evening.

Despite the long delays there was adventure in the new sights, and there were games to be played, new friendships to be struck up. The young teacher in charge of the girls' car next to Peter's was Maria Gorbochova and she knew all the old folk songs and accompanied herself on the mandolin. She taught the songs to the rest of them and every evening the sweet stringed notes and thin young voices swept over the fields and forests through which they moved.

On May 30 they arrived at Kotelnich and it was announced they would be there at least a week. Many trains were stranded in Vyatka on down the line and no one could move in any direction until the traffic mess was straightened out.

During their stay in Kotelnich the children and the teachers again made forays into the countryside to buy fresh food, but again were unsuccessful. They had pockets full of the new Soviet money and the peasants simply refused to take it. All their lives, and during the lives of their ancestors, the Romanoff ruble had been the medium of exchange and they didn't understand or trust this new money.

They had been in the village several days when the larger events of the outside world suddenly reached in to touch Peter. He and a friend were walking down the street on the edge of the village when two large men in foreign uniforms and speaking a strange language suddenly grabbed them and dragged them into a barracks. They were immediately surrounded by more men in the same type of unkempt uniforms who spoke to them in guttural voices.

After his initial fright had subsided Peter was able to understand the language was German. Then he understood that these were Austrian soldiers who were no longer prisoners of war. In the previous March the Soviet government had signed the treaty of Brest-Litovsk with Germany, ending hostilities and theoretically making German and Austrian prisoners free men. But in effect these Austrians were still captives of the village simply because there was no transport to take them home.

They questioned Peter eagerly about where he had been, where he was going, how he got food, what he knew about trains. The child had no encouraging information, and when he mentioned the six hundred idle and rusting engines which Fedor had counted, the men's faces fell and they drifted away from him and he was free to leave the barracks.

Finally, on the morning of June 7, the train moved slowly out of Kotelnich. Four days later it crawled along the banks of the River Gusev and at 1:00 P.M. entered Ekaterinburg and was shunted to a siding. This town marked their entry into Siberia. A few moments after the train had stopped, Maria Gorbochova came skipping into car No. 20 and called out, "We're going to lay over here several days, so let's all go sight-seeing!" There was eager agreement from Nikolay Borsouk and his charges.

"I've heard there's a wonderful museum here," she continued. "It has a great mineral collection and a display of stuffed animals. We can learn a lot about Siberia. Let's go!"

They all poured out of the train and lined up on the platform, two by two.

As the children marched into Ekaterinburg they sensed something strange. In previous towns the people on the streets had stared at them with open curiosity, often had come up to talk to them, sometimes had even given them little presents. But it was quite different here. There were some curious stares, but always quick, furtive, and no one approached them. And there were clusters of Red soldiers on almost every corner. The town seemed subdued and tense, as if the people were braced for some sort of awful event to take place.

Such an event was indeed destined to take place, and soon. After it happened there were to be great efforts made to hide it, even the name of the town was changed to Sverdlovsk, but all in vain. While the modern maps carry the name Sverdlovsk, the history books speak of Ekaterinburg.

Nikolay Borsouk marched briskly at the head of the column of children, Maria coming up at the rear. The tension in the town made Borsouk hesitate to ask directions. And for that reason he became lost and instead of arriving at the museum he led the children to the exact spot where the foreshadowed event was to take place.

They were passing through an upper-class residential neighborhood and came upon a particularly impressive house called Dom Ipatiev. It had been the resident of a leading merchant and was of rather grand proportions for a house in Siberia. It was of white brick, two stories tall and topped by an elaborate cornice of stone and ornamental iron. The windows had architectural eyebrows, and the first floor entrances were framed by Moorish arches. All around the building were Red Army soldiers, but not Russians. They were Letts, men brought all the way from Latvia for the duty of guarding the prisoners inside Dom Ipatiev—a fifty-year-old man with his wife, invalid son and four daughters.

The children slowed their steps and then stopped to stare at the structure. None of them had any previous knowledge of this building but from someone among them came the whispered words, "The Czar!" It ran through their ranks like a brush fire. "The Czar . . . the Czar!" Then it died out and the children stared with utter absorption.

What did they feel? None of their parents were Bolsheviks, to be sure, but few of them had been uncritical of Czar Nicholas II. This torpid, mystic, stubborn man had pretty well alienated the middle classes long before the Reds had sent him here, and the children looked at the building with neither veneration nor hostility, but with simple curiosity. If their stares could have penetrated the walls they might have felt pity.

The Czar and his family were confined to a sitting room and two bedrooms without sufficient beds. Their meals were swillish affairs without butter or coffee or salt. They were bullied and insulted by the habitually drunk guards, and whenever the Grand Duchess went to the lavatory she was escorted by the soldiers who lounged outside the door to shout obscenities and draw dirty pictures on the wall.

Nicholas lived through these indignities with quiet acceptance of his fate. He had always believed himself destined for tragedy. During his coronation the imperial chain had slipped from his neck and fallen to the ground, and he took this as an omen. He was really not surprised to find himself a prisoner at Ekaterinburg.

None of this could be seen and little of it guessed by the children staring at the outside of the building. And after several moments a Red soldier waved his rifle at them and shouted, "Get out! Get out of here!" They marched on down the street and finally found the museum. In their excitement over the stuffed wild animals they forgot all about the big white house.

Had they, by some chance, returned to stand outside Dom Ipatiev thirty-nine days later they would have heard the sound of gunshots in the basement as Nicholas and his family were being murdered. And had they returned to that same spot forty-two years later they would have seen an American U–2 reconnaissance plane shot out of the sky and the pilot, Francis Gary Powers, led off to Moscow for trial.

The Petrograd Children's Colony was to miss these events, but it was to make history of its own.

SEVEN

The three sections of the Petrograd Children's Colony, riding three separate trains, all arrived on the western Siberian plains and settled into various towns during the last week of June. The train carrying Peter and Fedor arrived at Koure on June 26. They had traveled five hundred miles from Petrograd and it had taken them a month and a day.

Koure was a village of 150 houses, one onion-topped church, a rather Byzantine courthouse and, on a hill above the Pyshma River, the rambling wooden hotel built to accommodate the visitors to the mineral springs—springs which had once been responsible for both the town's sulphurous smell and its prosperity. The smell remained, but the prosperity had gone. The war and the Revolution had ended the upper-class luxury of sulphur baths; it had just about ended the upper class. The town lay torpid and bitter, remembering the days when its shops sold the finest laces and the choicest wines. There was some stirring of hope when the children arrived, for surely they had money with them. A couple of souvenir shops re-opened, displaying bits of mineral and crudely carved wooden bears and picture postcards which showed the hotel at its grandest, with all the rocking chairs on the verandas occupied by ladies in leg-o'-mutton sleeves and gentlemen in cutaway coats and top hats.

Debarking from the train, the children trooped up the hill to the hotel which looked ghostly from long disuse. The teachers divided the children into work gangs to sweep and scrub the catacomb of rooms and the long verandas. The girls' dormitory was to be on the ground floor, the boys' on the second, the teachers scattered throughout both. By the second day routine set in: formal classes in the morning, free periods in the afternoon, songs and recitations and readings in the evening.

The afternoon free time was devoted to purchases, for few children could stand the weight of money in their pockets. They found the farmers reluctant to accept the new government rubles but eager for sugar. The children bought sugar in town, then traded it to the farmers for flour. Daily there was a line of children at the post office waiting to mail sacks of flour to Petrograd. And each week they received money from their parents, not only for their own needs, but to buy sugar to trade for more flour to be shipped back home. It was a quite satisfactory arrangement for all concerned.

The summer was mild on the eastern slope of the Urals and for most of the children, who had grown up in the city, it was all an exciting adventure. They swept over the country roads that were rutted by oxen and their carts, lost themselves in fields of grain that waved above their own tousled heads, explored the mysteries of the woods, dammed the streams to make waterfalls and grottos, caught the small wild creatures and made pets of them. After the darkness of Petrograd these warm, sunny days were tonic; they began to heal wounded minds and bodies.

On a sunny morning during the second week of July there was the sound of gunfire to the east. It was small arms fire and raggedly conducted. An accustomed ear could guess it came from troops in retreat, on the verge of rout. About noon stragglers began to enter Koure; they were Red soldiers, irregulars, partisans, some in uniform and some with parts of uniform and some with no uniform beyond the work clothes that identified their class and therefore their loyalties. Soon the trickle of retreat turned to a flood, and there was much milling about in the town square with wild rumors coming from all sides.

The children were confined to their hotel, though the teachers could not prevent them from crowding out on the open porches to watch the strange events. Questions arose that the teachers could not adequately answer, for there had been little communication from the war fronts. They all knew that a civil war was going on, that the White Russians were battling the Reds in the Ukraine, around Archangel, and at various places in Siberia, but they had thought Koure safe. But obviously the Whites were now advancing from the east.

That afternoon the hotel grounds became the front line. The children ran to their rooms and lay on the floor as bullets flew over the grounds and soldiers ran and shouted hoarsely. Then the line of battle swept on westward and they were suddenly in White territory instead of Red. But as they peeked fearfully out over the windowsills at the soldiers occupying the grounds, they saw a very strange sight—the White victors weren't Russians at all, but men in strange uniforms, men who turned out to be Czechs.

Late that day, after the gunfire had died down and the city firmly occupied by the Czechs, there was an important bustling, a coming and going of officers on the grounds of the hotel. The sun was low in the Ural Mountains when a line of men marched up the hill toward the hotel and as they drew near, it could be seen that they were tied together with ropes. They were Red Russian soldiers, prisoners of war. This fact was proclaimed by their uniforms and their bonds, but a look at their faces banished all claim to being warriors—they were young peasant boys and very scared.

The Czechs, who herded them along with bayonets, halted them in a ragged line just in front of the hotel veranda. From around the corner of the hotel marched a dozen Czech soldiers who took up position opposite the Russians and began to load their rifles. It finally became clear to the teachers inside the hotel that an execution was about to take place and they belatedly tried to get the children away from the windows. Horror has its own fascination and the children refused to budge.

The Czechs raised their rifles and fired a volley, and the children watched the result. One Russian soldier fell forward when shot, as if he were leaning toward the speeding bullet, eager for it. Another fell backward, as if he had decided to outrun the bullet but had stumbled. Another crumpled in a heap, as if all the fiber that held him erect had suddenly dissolved. One jerked into the air, arms and legs flung out in a single, grotesque ballet leap. One continued standing for a minute, then, with an expression of mild surprise, slowly sat down, then lay down, and was in seeming comfort.

Two days later the Czechs, leaving a small garrison behind, marched on in pursuit of the Reds. They got as far as the Urals and there, in the late summer, the front became stabilized with both sides digging in for the winter to come.

This came as stunning news to the children in Koure. It meant that they were trapped behind the battle lines and could not go home this September as planned. It meant facing the vicious Siberian winter without warm clothes and without the ability to buy any (the Soviet ruble was outlawed in White territory). They would have to depend upon the mercy, or generosity, or greed, of the countryside.

The children began to sell their personal possessions, and when these were gone they sold the sheets on their beds, and then the blankets. When there was nothing left, they spread out in the town and countryside in an effort to ingratiate themselves with a family and win a meal. The people of Koure were generous with the children as long as there was extra food, but the occupying armies were demanding more and more of it and there was a shortage of manpower to harvest the fields already planted.

Finally the village was sick to death of the children who had turned into little beggars, and then into little thieves, and all doors were shut against them.

There loomed now another desperate problem—the approach of winter. There was no method of heating the old hotel which had been constructed only for summer occupancy, and to remain any longer was impossible. The teachers conferred for many desperate hours without being able to reach a decision. To go west was to head right into the battle lines; to go east was to be lost deeper in Siberia. And they could not stay where they were. As frightening as the prospect was, they decided to go east.

They started out on a grey October morning when all the world seemed to be dying. Their ragged line came down the hill and through the village where the doors and windows were shut against them. Those townspeople who peeked out to watch felt pity and guilt, and relief.

By noon the wavering column had gone ten miles and could go no farther. The children's thin bodies sprawled exhausted on the roadside, looking like battle casualties. The teachers had set as their goal the town of Tyumen, and it was two hundred miles away!

An hour went by in silence and apathy. Could the children be roused now for another effort? If so, it could bring no more than another five miles. It seemed hardly worth it.

The thin, melancholy wail of a train whistle drifted to them across the dreary land. Maria Gorbochova suddenly jumped to her feet and began to yell excitedly. She pointed across a field where, two hundred yards away, a pair of steel rails could be seen running from horizon to horizon. "Everybody on the railroad track. Quick . . . quick! On the railroad track. Run for it!"

Slowly, painfully, like a wounded animal, the Colony stirred and moved and began to flow across the field. Soon it covered the tracks, submerging them like a flood. The train came into view, whistled wildly but slowed and came to a shuddering stop. The children swarmed over it, occupying coaches and boxcars, and when those were filled, the roofs. The train crew could no more repel them than a farmer could drive off a plague of locusts.

At last the train started up again, panting under its new burden. The children who clung to it were as tired and hungry as before, but their hearts stirred with hope. In a disintegrating world the mere fact of motion seemed to promise safety.

Then they came to Tyumen and the train stopped at the outskirts and the conductor insisted that the children get off. It was night and difficult to see, but they had stumbled along a rutted street for less than a hundred yards when they came to an abandoned house and occupied it.

Tyumen was larger than Koure and therefore presented more devious ways in which fuel and food could be found. The children were a curiosity to the town in the beginning, but not for long, and soon the doors were shut against them just as they had been in Koure.

Thus was the story told by Peter to the old farmer and his wife. When he finished speaking the old woman blew her nose loudly and insisted that they eat more pancakes, which they could not do. The old man pulled thoughtfully on his beard for a few moments, exchanged glances with his wife, then spoke.

"If you will help with the work and stay for the spring planting, you can live with us over the winter."

The two boys looked at each other. These were the very words they had hoped to hear, but now, strangely, they didn't welcome them. They remembered Maria Gorbochova and all their friends, and they felt a tie that was stronger than any logic.

"Thank you," Peter said, "but we'll buy the bread and get started back to Tyumen."

The bread brought back by Peter and Fedor was welcome, but when cut into tiny pieces and distributed it assuaged no one's hunger. Day by day the situation grew more desperate. Farmers who initially gave bread or sold it stopped doing so. Moreover, the children became too weak even to go into the countryside in search. Throughout the long hours of the grey days they lay huddled around the stoves and fireplaces that were consuming the very structure that housed them. There were no quarrels among the children, no weeping, for apathy had taken over.

On Monday of the second week of January the front door of the dying house was briskly opened and banged shut and there appeared a man. The children looked up at him in wonder, for they had not seen such a man for a long time. He was well fed. And clean. His uniform fit him smartly and was without stains. His whole being spoke of the kind of security of health they had almost forgotten existed.

Maria climbed to her feet and stood before him. He said, "My name is Charles Colles and I'm from the American Red Cross. I've been searching for you."

"Searching . . . for *us?*" Maria said in a disbelieving voice. They had been forgotten by the world, she was sure. What could this apparition mean?

The man began inspecting the house room by room, while Maria and Borsouk and the other teachers trailed along behind him and exchanged dazed looks. The man was talking, half to himself and half to them. "Must bathe the children, burn their clothing and disinfect the entire house. Can't take a chance on typhus. I can have a doctor and several nurses here by tomorrow. The new clothing is warehoused in Omsk . . . have to truck it here. Also by tomorrow, I should think. Start a high protein diet at once, also vitamin supplements."

He turned around to face them and said, "Call the children together and I'll say a few words."

There was no need, for the children were already gathered around him, their eyes wide with wonder.

"The American people are going to take care of you," he said to them. "You're going to have warm new clothes and all the food you can eat and plenty of firewood to keep you warm. But I want you to do something in repayment; I want you to be good citizens. No more roaming the streets to beg and steal.

And when we are able to get you some books, you must resume your studies. I'll come and see you every week because I am the boss and you must do what I tell you to do. I am also your friend."

When he finished speaking there was the sound of weeping. It was Maria Gorbochova. She had been the boss for too long and beyond her strength. She wept in relief that stronger shoulders had taken the burden.

Throughout January and early February 1919 the Red Cross found and brought together the various bands of Petrograd children. By March 1919 Colles had supervision of 188 children at Tyumen, 206 at Shadrinsk, and 176 at Irbit. Red Cross Field Directors Mr. and Mrs. A. J. Snow had supervision of 118 children in Petropavlovsk, 81 at Kurgan, 103 at Troitsk and 95 at Ouiskaia.

For the moment death had been cheated.

EIGHT

With the proper food and medicines the young bodies mended quickly and spirits rose in direct ratio to health. In a land convulsed by war and disease, the Petrograd children's colonies became tiny oases of sanity and hope. All because the Americans had reached out over thousands of miles of desolation to enfold them.

Yet the children were not to escape their time entirely. As spring arrived the tempo of the civil war increased and the White military position began to deteriorate. By yards, and then by miles, the battlefront moved eastward until it threatened the cities where the children were living.

The Red Cross was plunged into a policy crisis. There were those who advised that the children simply be abandoned, but this was stoutly opposed by Riley Allen. He maintained that having saved these children from death, the Red Cross was committed to keeping them alive and returning them to their parents. To let the war front engulf them was unthinkable, for there would be neither food nor transport behind the Red lines and they could not survive another such experience.

Allen's solution? He boldly proposed that they all be gathered up and brought back to the comparative safety of Vladi-vostok. Here they could be housed and protected by the Americans until the civil war was ended and the Trans-Siberian Railway repaired and operating back to Petrograd. Allen held firm to his simple principle that whoever won the war, Red or White, the children should be reunited with their parents.

He admitted that such an undertaking was fraught with troubles and dangers, but he insisted there was no other honorable and humanitarian course. Teusler had returned to his hospital in Tokyo, leaving Allen acting commissioner. The young newspaperman had the full burden of responsibility but he did not falter under it. He was available to all men, listened to all opinions, but once having reached his own, he was adamant. The children *had* to be saved.

After much soul-searching, A.R.C. headquarters in Washington sustained him. He organized three rescue trains, stocked them with doctors and nurses and food and medicine, put them on the tracks and sent them toward the Urals. It was July 1919.

Carl Myers was in charge of the first rescue train to move. He had been carefully chosen for the job, which would demand both toughness and compassion. This twenty-eight-year-old native of Minneapolis was a square man with a square face and a broad, easy smile. He was a director of Red Cross Camp Service, which meant his job was to console the homesick, divert the bored, comfort the ill. He was a boxing coach, an actor with a large repertoire of recitations, a singer with a strong baritone voice, a magician with a bag of tricks. There was about him an aura of cheerful, masculine competence. He was the perfect father image for children who were lost and scared.

The children, being brought together at various railway terminals, were plunged into the chaos of a military machine in defeat. Typical of all stations was the one at Omsk. Kolchak's soldiers wandered about aimlessly, their faces haggard and apathetic. Open freight cars on sidings were piled with

kitchen equipment and field pieces and small arms, all awaiting a clear track for evacuation eastward. The wounded
crawled, or merely lay on the platform unheeded. There were
a number of boxcars of Bolshevik prisoners, their arms extended through the tiny windows under the eaves in supplica-
tion for a cup of water or a crust of bread. There was the fetid
atmosphere of bestiality and decay.

And into it came the children. They were lost and fright-
ened, not just from the scene before them, but from the
knowledge that they were not being taken home to their parents as they'd hoped, but were being sent to the very farthest
limits of Siberia.

The children were divided up in the various cars according
to age, and the older ones according to sex. Carl Myers had a
little speech he made in each car as he visited them that first
evening. To the older groups he said, "You are going to have to
be very grown up and help us with the smaller children. We're
going to be together for a long time and so we're going to have
to love each other. If we all started to quarrel in this small
space, you can see what a lot of trouble we would have . . .
no fun at all."

And to the smaller children, gathered in a circle at his feet,
he said, "Your mothers and fathers are searching for you, and
we're searching for them. We'll find each other pretty soon.
But in the meantime we're going to have lessons and we're
going to have games and we'll have a nice long trip and see
wonderful sights. There's going to be plenty of food, and
plenty of nice clothes and we're going to be very happy together. So now, let's all sing a song and then to bed."

The passage of this big, gentle man from coach to coach
calmed and soothed and reassured. That night at bedtime
there were a few secret tears, but not many.

In the long succession of days that followed, Myers introduced the Russian children to magic tricks, to songs and stories
about America, to such nonsense games as Simon Says, to calisthenics when the train was in motion, to impromptu track

meets when the train was standing still. And it stood still a good share of the time.

The war front was rapidly disintegrating behind them, and the Red partisans were making more and more raids in front of them. Frequently the track was torn up, and they had to wait for repairs. More frequently they ran out of fuel for the engine and had to hunt the countryside for wood. They couldn't cut and burn green wood, so they negotiated with the peasants for seasoned fence posts.

The peasants refused to take Kolchak rubles, or Romanoff rubles, or Soviet rubles. Myers had foreseen this impasse and brought with him a number of bolts of yard goods. Each time the train wheezed to a stop, out of fire and out of steam, Myers hacked off a few yards of cloth and sent the train crew out to buy the necessary fuel. Sometimes they would return within an hour or so, sometimes it took a day, but always the wood was found and always the train crept forward.

NINE

In the American Red Cross compound in Vladivostok there was intense activity. To bring eight hundred children safely into a city as divided and strife torn and hungry as this was a formidable undertaking. Perhaps in all the world the only organization that would have attempted it was the Red Cross, and even here it required the presence of a special man—Riley Allen.

By now he was in complete charge of the Siberian Commission and it was his optimism, his determination, his selflessness, his patience, his humor, that set the tone of the organization. Also, he was undeniably lucky in his subordinates.

Throughout the summer of 1919, while they were preparing to receive the children, Allen came to depend more and more upon two of his associates. One of them was a squarish, lusty woman in her thirties who laughed easily and had a thirst for adventure. Her name was Hannah Brain Campbell and, with her husband and two small children, she had suddenly appeared out of the wilds of Siberia to volunteer her services. Desperately shorthanded, Allen accepted her offer. Within a week everyone in Barracks No. 7 was calling her "Mother

Campbell" and Allen began to appreciate what Providence
had sent him. And certainly she had been sent to Vladivostok
by a most circuitous route.

Hannah and Charles Campbell had originally been chicken
farmers in New Jersey but the lure of gold and adventure drew
them to Alaska. They had little success and when they heard
there was much yellow richness east of Lake Baikal they
packed up their two children (ages eight and three) and
headed into Siberia.

This was the autumn of 1917, a time of war, revolution and
civil war. But these events had been confined to European
Russia and had not penetrated to the mountain cabin the
Campbells had built by the side of a stream in Siberia. Along
with Charles's cousin, who had joined them, their complete
preoccupation was with gold. They found it, but they also
found that the bleak land did not easily surrender its treasure.
The yellow stuff was in earth frozen to the texture of granite,
and no pickaxe could loosen it.

Heavy equipment had to be brought in by horse and sled. It
consisted of a wood-fired boiler to which was attached a dozen
long hoses that ended in iron "steam points." These points,
hollow rods perforated with holes, were driven into the frozen
ground and left there overnight to force steam into the frost
and ice. By morning the ground would be thawed enough to
be dug and carted to the stream and panned for its gold.

Laboriously they worked at this all through the winter of
1917–18, and in the Siberian darkness and cold they were
warmed by the growing bags of gold. But then events in
Petrograd reached out and touched them. Hannah Campbell
was to need all her resilience of spirit to face this remote and
tiny backlash of the Revolution.

It was on a March afternoon. Charles Campbell and his
cousin were shoveling the chunks of earth into wheelbarrows
for the trip to the stream. Hannah was cleaning the ashes out
of the firebox of the steam boiler in preparation for laying a

new fire. There came to them the creak of snow underfoot and they looked up to see a half-dozen men approaching them.

There was nothing menacing, these were villagers they had all seen before, and yet there was something new about the way they walked, a purposefulness, a touch of self-conscious arrogance. They stopped before the boiler and stood for a moment in a silent group. Finally one of them stepped forward, the spokesman, the leader. He was the village barber.

He wore his new authority uneasily and the fingers on his right hand twitched, as if they still held a pair of scissors. He bowed slightly and said, "Greetings."

"Hello," Charles Campbell replied. Both he and his wife had learned enough Russian for ordinary conversations.

"I have the honor to inform you," said the barber, becoming more and more formal, "that this land and its gold now belongs to the people."

The Americans stared at him, puzzled. They had heard rumors of the revolutionary events to the west, but they had to fit these words into what they had heard. After a moment Charles said, "This land belongs to farmer Karpoff and we have leased the mineral rights from him."

The barber shook his head. "It belongs now to all the people. Not just to Karpoff but all the people. Everything belongs to all the people."

Hannah Campbell stepped beside her husband. "You mean," she said, "you now want us to lease it from you folks?"

This was, apparently, a new idea to the barber and he turned to consult his committee. There was an extended and rather heated discussion conducted in whispers. At last the barber turned back and said, "The people's land cannot be leased."

"Well, what in hell you going to do with it?" Charles Campbell cried, exasperated.

Again there was a conference. The barber said, "You can stay here and mine the gold but you must share it with the people."

Campbell looked at the six men before him and made a
mental calculation. "Share it how many ways?" he asked.

"With all the people," the barber said, sweeping his arm
across the horizon.

"With every Russian in the country?" Campbell asked, disbelieving.

"All the people."

"There's over a hundred million Russians!" He pointed a
shaking finger at the pile of gold-bearing earth beside the
frozen stream. "You divide that a hundred million ways and
how much do you think *you*'ll get? I'll get?"

The barber was at a loss how to answer this and he retreated
into stern dignity. "Lenin says that it belongs to all the people.
That is the socialist way."

The argument ran on for half an hour, but there was no real
interchange of thoughts; there was no room for negotiation or
compromise. They were all caught in the vice of a logic beyond their comprehension or control. Hannah was the first to
realize the futility. Perhaps her husband perceived it as soon,
but she had the strength to accept it first.

She put her hand on his arm and said gently, "It's no use,
Dad." Then she turned to the barber and said, "We'll go. You'll
allow us to take our own possessions, of course."

"Not the mining equipment," he said. "We will need that."

The Campbells had no further need of the boiler and the
steam points. She said to her husband, "I'll go pack."

The next morning they left camp, all their possessions piled
on two sleds. Just before snapping the whips over the horses'
heads Charles and his cousin walked slowly and contempla-
tively around the pile of gold they had accumulated. It was all
there, every dream a man could possibly dream, a fingertip
away!

Hannah Campbell did not join them in this last bitter rite;
she had the children to care for. When Elizabeth and Charles,
Junior, were secure on the sled, wrapped in furs, she called to

the men and they came reluctantly to start the journey southward and east.

They traveled on sleds for forty miles and came to a small
mining community that was full of other refugees from the
new Socialism. A dozen of them banded together and built a
flat-bottomed scow and launched themselves upon a large
stream flowing east. A week later they came to the Zeya River
and were there able to board a steamer that took them to
Blagoveshchensk, a town that was notable for the fact that it
had a single line of track connecting to the Trans-Siberian
Railway.

The cousin decided to go on south to Shanghai but the
Campbells hoped for Vladivostok where they could find passage home to America. The four of them found room in a
boxcar and sat on the floor to begin a long and jolting trip.
Many times in the following weeks they were forced to change
trains, but each new boxcar seemed slower, seemed to be side-
tracked for longer periods than the previous one.

At least the Campbells had a destination, few among their
fellow passengers did. Aristocrats, peasants, students, merchants, they were all huddled together in the misery of hunger
and lostness. There was no fare charged on the trains because
the owners were no longer around to demand it. The railroad
continued to run from momentum, from habit, because the
engineers and conductors didn't know what to do except their
jobs. And so the passengers just shuttled back and forth, looking for lost children or lost parents or lost friends, lost hope.
Every woman seemed to carry a pack of her most precious
things: the lock of a child's hair, the family hand-embroidered
sheets, a samovar, a faded picture, a book. And always, closely
guarded, some sour bread.

Some of these families had been traveling over the same
track for weeks and months, dumbly submitting to whatever
fate came along. They had lost the power to make decisions, to
plan for themselves.

Late one afternoon the train came to a sudden, shuddering

stop just before a tunnel through a small mountain. "Every-body out who's going to Vladivostok!" shouted the conductor. "There's a Czech military train coming toward us and we're going to reverse engine. Hurry . . . out . . . out!"

The Campbells and a number of other passengers climbed out but before the train could start up again, the Czech mili-tary train emerged from the tunnel and everybody froze. The Czechs had an engine and four gondola cars out of which poked rifles and machine guns. The sight was too much for a Chinese man standing near the Campbells and he broke and ran. There was a burst of machine gun fire from the train and he fell, shot through the chest. No one else moved.

The train stopped and a Czech officer jumped down and walked toward them. He paused in front of the Campbells and said in English, "I see you are Americans."

"How did you know?" exclaimed Hannah, hoping the relief in her voice was not unfounded.

The officer pointed down to Charles, Junior. The three-year-old clutched a small American flag in his hand. Neither parent could remember having seen it before, could not imagine where he had picked it up. It was all a minor miracle, though major enough at the moment.

"We're not going to hurt anyone," the Czech said. He had either forgotten or did not count the dead Chinese. "We have to search your train for Bolsheviks. Do any of you have in-formation you can give me?"

No one had any information.

The train was searched and no Reds found. The officer waved them forward, they were free to proceed to Vladivos-tok. But there was concern among the crew and finally the conductor came forth with a bit of information he apparently just remembered. The tunnel was about to be blown up. Reds were in the mountain and they planned to blow up the tunnel as soon as the Czechs were through it, thus cutting off their return to Vladivostok.

The officer called a platoon of men down from the train and

sent them on foot up over the mountain to prevent any such action. Then he waved the freight forward.

The engineer hesitated to pull the throttle. "Your men may not get there in time," he objected. "The tunnel may be blown up with my train inside."

"Ha!" the Czech scoffed. "It takes the Russians a long time to do anything. You have plenty of time."

The Campbells and their fellow passengers climbed back into the boxcar and the train rolled. They seemed forever in the dark and tomb-like tunnel and each moment expected to hear the explosions that would forever seal them in. But none came. The Czech officer had been right. They rolled out into the sunshine and on southward.

Late that night, two and a half months after leaving the gold mine, their boxcar was shunted onto a siding in the big marshaling yards at Vladivostok. The next morning a brakeman pounded on the side of the car and told them to get out. As they dropped painfully to the cinder track the clear, silvery note of a bugle cut through the air. They looked down at the harbor and there was a great battleship with her sailors, dressed in immaculate white, lined up on deck as a flag was being run up. The flag ran up limp, but as it reached the top of the stern flagstaff a breeze caught it, spanked it out into a dazzling red, white and blue. The ship was the U.S.S. *Brooklyn.*

The Campbells had no idea there was an American within thousands of miles. Now at last, they clutched their children hard against them and wept.

They had come to Vladivostok to book passage home, but when they saw the American Red Cross headquarters, they volunteered and were gratefully accepted. Charles was placed in charge of the warehouse, Hannah in charge of Barracks No. 7.

The other associate upon whom Allen particularly depended was a twenty-six-year-old accountant named Burle Bramhall. He had volunteered in Seattle, and with thirty-two other Red

Cross workers had come across the Pacific on the *Kashima Maru*. If he stood out from the others during that voyage it was only because of his reticence. He had a tall, slender body topped by a slender face. He looked at the world from heavy-lidded and rather measuring eyes.

Some people, when first meeting him, thought him stuck-up. But after closer acquaintance they concluded he was shy. Neither the first nor the second impression was entirely true; the core of the man was preoccupation with work. He enjoyed a party; he danced with a stately stride and he took a drink and he told jokes in a quiet and wry manner, but his pleasure was to plan a job and then to do it. A sense of duty was the gyro within this man, and he was absolutely unflappable. Riley Allen could not have had a better assistant during the turbulence ahead.

Soon after Bramhall's arrival there was a financial crisis. To operate its hospitals and pay for goods and services, the Red Cross had purchased large amounts of Kerensky rubles which Kolchak had converted to his regime's official use. Now that the war front was disintegrating, these rubles were depreciating rapidly and in one week's time went from 300 per American dollar to 3,000 per dollar. To save its investment the Red Cross had somehow to convert its Russian money to some suitable currency with minimum loss. The Chinese mex was such a unit. The only way to change rubles for mex, however, was to go to Harbin, Manchuria, where the money changers had shops. It was obviously a trip for a man of financial knowledge and strong nerves. Bramhall was such a man.

Hazardous as it was, the only way to get to Harbin was by the Trans-Siberian Railway, so Bramhall requisitioned a small boxcar, stocked it with a stove and food and with a young Hungarian P.O.W. who spoke Chinese, attached the car to a train going west. As he boarded the car he carried an ordinary-looking briefcase that contained $250,000 in Kerensky rubles. He hoped his mission was secret, for a human life went a good deal cheaper.

He arrived in Harbin without incident and found the street of the money changers. It was about two blocks long and contained shops on each side. The process of negotiation was a long one. He would go into a shop, display as much as 10,000 rubles and ask for an exchange rate into mex. If it was too low he'd go to the next shop. Sometimes he'd be called back at the first shop, sometimes not. He could never dispose of more than 10,000 to a changer, and even after the rate had been agreed upon, the changer would inspect each bill with a magnifying glass. If he found so much as a pinhole, that bill would be declared defective and a whole new rate of exchange had to be negotiated for it. It took Bramhall ten days to change all the rubles into mex. Then he began the return trip to Vladivostok, the highly negotiable Chinese money stuffed into his case.

If the trip up to Harbin had been dangerous, the trip back down was doubly so because any foreigner leaving the city of money changers was presumed to have pockets full of mex. Bramhall and his translator ate and slept in the boxcar for three days before they finally got out of Manchuria and into the Russian border village of Grodekovo. It was here that the Japanese took over control of the railroad.

The train arrived in the village at midmorning and by noon it had not moved. There was no loading or unloading of freight from the other boxcars, nothing to indicate that the track ahead was not clear; they were just unaccountably stalled. Perhaps it was not so unaccountable, Bramhall decided, for the Japanese soldiers kept glancing at his boxcar. They seemed to be speculating on what he carried. Perhaps they were trying to decide whether they dared to conduct a search and confiscation. Bramhall decided that sitting and waiting for them to make the first move would not do.

"Stephen," he said to his Hungarian companion, "you speak Japanese. Go into the station there and demand an official explanation of the delay."

Stephen climbed down the iron ladder that hung beneath the boxcar's open door and disappeared into the station.

Bramhall observed that several Japanese soldiers followed him in. A few moments later angry shouts emerged from the small station, then the sounds of a fight. Stephen was in trouble. Bramhall glanced anxiously at the corner of the boxcar where the briefcase was hidden beneath a clutter of pots and pans. He had established a rule that at no time should both of them be out of the boxcar, out of sight of the money. But he couldn't abandon the man to the Japanese if he was in trouble. Bramhall jumped down to the ground and ran into the station to find Stephen lying on the floor, trying to protect himself from the blows and kicks of a circle of Japanese soldiers.

Bramhall was tall even by American standards and he towered over the Japanese. Also, he had the advantage of surprise, for none of the soldiers had seen him enter. With a great shout he waded into the middle of the circle, bowling over two of the soldiers, pulled Stephen to his feet and marched him out the door and toward the boxcar.

"What did they want?" Bramhall demanded.

"I don't know . . . I . . . I couldn't understand," Stephen mumbled.

"They wanted to know if we carried money. What did you tell them?"

"I didn't tell them anything," Stephen cried. "Before God!"

They came to the boxcar, Bramhall boosted him up and followed. Then, for the first time, he looked back. The soldiers, six of them, had come out of the station and were now standing with heads together, talking in excited tones. Bramhall walked to his duffel bag where he got out his sidearm, strapped it to his belt and walked back to stand in the open door.

The soldiers had made up their minds and were now coming toward the boxcar. One of them grabbed the bottom rung of the ladder and began to climb. When his head appeared above the floor of the boxcar, Bramhall pulled back his heavy booted foot and kicked him in the chin. The man screamed, fell backward to the ground and lay there, moaning. His comrades looked down at him for a moment, and then they looked back up at Bramhall and their faces held the most extraordinary expressions. They were smiling. And then they bowed. They discovered for the first time that the gentleman wore the uniform of the American Red Cross. They were so sorry to have disturbed him. They picked up the soldier who had been kicked and marched away. Minutes later the train started up and by the end of the day Bramhall and the money were safely back in Barracks No. 7.

CHAPTER

TEN

In the middle of Vladivostok's Bay of the Golden Horn there was a rocky outcropping named Russian Island. On it were massive stone barracks that had once housed the men of the Czar's fleet, but which now stood vacant. Here, it seemed to Allen, was the perfect place to quarter the Petrograd children when they arrived. With a minimum of repair to kitchens and sanitary facilities the island could receive the children and keep them safe from the chaos of the city.

What Allen wanted Allen generally got, but in this case the most delicate and subtle negotiations were required. No one in Vladivostok was quite sure who had title to the island now that the Czar was dead, and there were many who coveted the strategically placed rock. But of all the contenders, Allen's patience and determination were the strongest and by July he had obtained a lease and sent a task force of carpenters and plumbers to repair the grim old buildings.

Mother Campbell became the straw boss on the job, directing the arrangement of the kitchen, the partitioning off of classrooms and recreation rooms, the collection of books and toys and pictures. All this was in addition to her duties in

Barracks No. 7, where she was maître d', room clerk, house-keeper, social director, chaperone, banker, confidante and advisor.

She was a strong believer in the therapy of laughter and food and she supplied the two in generous amounts. The young Red Cross volunteers who arrived from America with some apprehension found a warm and welcoming atmosphere had been created by Mother Campbell. Her method of operation was made clear to Riley Allen the first week she was on the job. He had said to her:

"Mother Campbell, ten nurses are arriving from America tomorrow on the *Empress of Japan*. Can we find room for them?"

The barracks was already crowded with close to three hundred but that didn't faze Mother Campbell. "We'll squeeze them in," she said, "but, my goodness, what am I going to do for turkeys? I'll have to leave for the market right now. They're awful hard to find."

"You must have plenty of food in the kitchen. Why do you bother about turkey?" Riley asked.

"Because those girls will be far from home in a foreign land, that's why. The food on that ship is awful and they'll be homesick and there'll be nothing like a traditional American meal of turkey and pumpkin pie to cheer them up. And by golly, they're going to have it."

They did have it, and she was quite right about its effect upon the girls' morale. They arrived bedraggled and feeling lost, but the meal lifted their spirits. Not just because it was American food, but because there was a "mother" who worried about them and planned for them.

When she took a three-day trip to Harbin to visit some friends, she left a Korean assistant named Mig Park in charge of the dining room. When she returned he burst out, "Mother, don't you never leave me in charge of this damn place any more."

"What happened?"

"It was that big Spangler, the railroad man."

He referred to a member of the Russian Railway Service Corps, a group of American railway men from the Great Northern and Northern Pacific railways who had volunteered to serve under the Army Engineers in an effort to restore the efficiency of the crippled Trans-Siberian. They worked as telegraphers and dispatchers, and there were 288 of them strung out along the all but dismembered road. When they were in Vladivostok they ate and slept at Barracks No. 7.

"What did Spangler do?" Mother Campbell demanded of Mig Park.

"Well, we had hamburger for dinner last night . . ."

"Oh, lordy," she moaned, "I told you never to serve Sam Spangler ground-up meat."

"I forgot."

"What'd he do?"

"He jumped up from the table and shouted at the top of his voice, 'I can chew my own meat!' Then he threw his plate down on the table and it spilled all over everybody and he walked out. Somebody reported it to Major Strong and now there's bad trouble."

Mother Campbell sighed. "I'll go see the Major, but he's a stiff one and I don't cotton to him much."

Major Strong of the Engineers received Mother Campbell and said, "I'm ordering Lieutenant Spangler out of Barracks No. 7."

"Well, now, isn't that a bit harsh, Major? He won't find quarters as good and . . ."

"He was guilty of conduct unbecoming an officer," the Major replied icily.

"It seems to me he was guilty of conduct of a man who just can't stand ground-up meat. It was my fault for ever letting it be served to him."

"That's ridiculous!"

"All I'm asking, Major, is that you let me take care of the situation. Give me a chance before you throw him out."

She was given her chance, though with little graciousness.

That afternoon she placed herself in the recreation room where she knew she'd meet Spangler. He came in and walked directly up to her, glowering. They faced each other for a moment, then she began to laugh.

"You big galoot!" she cried, laughing harder.

Now he laughed, too. Both of them roared.

Later Major Strong demanded a report. "Oh," she said, "everything is fine."

"What did you do?" he insisted.

"I laughed at him, that's all."

"Is he going to eat his food properly?" the Major demanded.

"Oh yes, sir. Very properly."

And Spangler did. Mother Campbell was careful to see that he was never again served ground-up meat.

The allocation of sleeping space can sometimes be a problem, as any hotel manager can testify. Generally Mother Campbell's guests were too preoccupied with their jobs to worry about the placement of their cots, but Dr. Igor Rubansky was the exception. He had been working in a refugee camp outside Vladivostok and developed a reputation as a complainer. He was being returned to the United States and appeared in Barracks No. 7 to await his ship.

"I've been having a very bad time of it," he said to Mother Campbell, "and I need a good rest. Please put me in a private room."

"Doc, we don't have any private rooms here."

"Then put me in the quietest room you have. I must get rest."

"Quiet?" she grinned at him. "With three hundred people tucked in, sometimes these windows rattle with the snores."

"Do the best you can for me." He gave her a suffering smile.

"I'm not even sure I've got a bed for you, but come on. We'll have a look."

The only bed left in the entire structure was in the "bullpen," a corner of a large area which contained eighteen cots and eighteen bureaus, seventeen of which were occupied.

"Oh no, I couldn't sleep here," Rubansky said.

"Then you'd better find another hotel," she said, and walked away.

That night she was just closing up the canteen on the first floor at about eleven o'clock when a strapping warehouseman named Jake Adano marched up to her, his face dark with anger.

"Mother Campbell," he growled, "I want you to come with me."

She closed the canteen and followed him, suspecting that they were headed for the bullpen. They were. When they arrived, Jake waved his arm and cried, "Take a look at that, I ask ya!"

Dr. Rubansky had appropriated for himself one-quarter of the area, pushing the other cots out of the way and building around himself a wall of clothes bureaus. He sat upright in his cot, defiantly peering over the barricade. A dozen of his room-mates stood together, glowering but indecisive.

Mother Campbell said briskly to them, "Don't just stand there. Help me get this room back in order."

Together they dismantled the wall, pushed the cots and the bureaus back into place and finally Dr. Rubansky occupied one-eighteenth of the area instead of one-quarter.

"One more thing, Mother Campbell," Jake said as she was about to go. "What about the window? We want it open, he wants it shut."

She thought a moment, then said, "I look at it this way. We may be in Russia, but Barracks No. 7 is a piece of the United States of America. And in America the majority always rules."

The following morning she met Dr. Rubansky coming down the stairs and beneath one eye was a bruise rapidly turning black and blue. "What happened, Doc?" she demanded.

He muttered, "I fell down." Then he brushed on past her.

When she went into the dining hall at breakfast time she marched down the tables until she came to Jake Adano. She grabbed up his right hand to examine it and found his knuckles reddened. "Jake . . . !" she admonished.

"We voted on it, Mother Campbell," he said quickly. "We voted that I should punch him one. And you yourself said that the majority should rule."

During the staff meeting later that morning Riley Allen asked, "Mother Campbell, what happened in the bullpen last night?"

"You had a complaint?" she asked.

"No, but I've heard rumors."

She grinned. "Then don't bother about it. Nothing happened but a little democracy. And democracy never hurt anybody . . . not for long."

Since these were young men and young women who lived in Barracks No. 7, sex was bound to become something of a problem. Mother Campbell had a simple and forthright attitude toward the whole thing; she treated Red Cross girls as if they were her own daughters, which meant that she wanted them to have a good time and she did not want them to get pregnant or sustain a broken heart.

They brought their problems to her. A girl would say, "I think he got too fresh last night. What should I do?"

"Stop going out with him," she'd say. "There's three boys to every girl here, so you have plenty of chance to choose a nice one. Give the fresh ones the go-by."

And when serious romance developed, Mother Campbell moved in with the stern words: "Don't decide anything about marriage here. You'll be going home soon and things may look quite different back in the U. S. A. For heaven's sake, wait until you get home!"

All this was sound advice but when it ran counter to the surge of human biology it did not always prevail. Mother Campbell searched for a way of making a stronger impression on her charges. She found it, strangely, from a colonel serving in Army Intelligence. His name was Robert Eichelberger and years later in World War II he was to become a famous general.

Mother Campbell always held a dance in the recreation hall on Saturday nights and her friend Eichelberger dropped in on one of them. Since there were many more men than women, there was no such thing as a wallflower. No matter how fat and homely a girl might be, she was constantly in demand as a dancing partner.

The Colonel stood beside Mother Campbell and watched the couples swirling around the floor to the music of an ancient gramophone, and he said wryly, "I suppose it's impossible to get some of those girls to understand that it's not their personal attraction that makes them so damn popular, but the geographical position."

Mother Campbell let out a hoot, slapped her hip and cried, "Colonel Ike, you've just given me a great idea. You ought to get a medal for it."

The next afternoon she held a tea for all the girls and when they had gathered together she gave them a little talk. "I want you to know what Colonel Ike said last night." After she had repeated the conversation she said, "That is going to be our secret code word—geographical position."

Thereafter, whenever she saw one of her girls spooning with a little too much heat, she'd drift by and say out of the corner of her mouth, "Gladys, don't forget your geographical position."

This always sent the girl into a fit of giggles, and almost always broke the spell that the boy had so hopefully created.

As the summer of 1919 passed and the Red Cross braced itself for the arrival of the children, Allen occasionally speculated on what the coming job would be like if there were no Mother Campbell. He found it painful to imagine.

ELEVEN

The Children's Colony arrived in Vladivostok on three different trains during the first week of September 1919 and it was a time of great excitement and some confusion. None of them had been in this Asian city before and they sought out its uniqueness with eager eyes. There was one, however, for whom the arrival produced a profound experience that had nothing to do with architecture or geography. Her name was Tatjana Nikolenko.

Tatjana Nikolenko was one of the children of the Colony that had spent the summer in Petropavlovsk. She was twelve years old and so fair of skin and hair that she seemed always to move in a nimbus of sunlight. Her face was heart-shaped with high and widely separated cheekbones, and it held an expression of grave serenity. She was the recipient of more girlish confidences than anybody else in her group, for she was never shocked, never repeated what was told her, and was always interested in the revelations.

She had only one drawback as a confidante—her brother Gregorii was always with her. But since Gregorii was only three and had such obvious disinterest in the whispered conversations that went on above his head, the girls soon learned to accept him and ignore him. And if there was something really important to talk about, Tatjana could be prevailed upon to send Gregorii off to play at a distance, out of hearing but not out of sight.

When they had left Petrograd, Tatjana's mother had said, "Don't let Gregorii out of your sight," and she had accepted the command quite literally. The child slept on a cot next to her when cots were available, on the ground next to her when there were no cots. He walked beside her until he was tired, and then she carried him. When in her arms, his feet dangled almost to her knees and he seemed a great burden, but she never complained.

She had a great sense of family loyalty and duty. Also, she had infinite patience. The teachers shook their heads and said to each other, "What a wonderful little mother Tatjana is."

Her popularity could be judged by the fact that when the teachers developed the habit of publicly using her conduct as an example for the others, the girls did not hate her. They knew that Tatjana did not try to act better, did not even think that she acted better. It was just that she *was* better and it gave her no cause for airs. Nobody expected to be like Tatjana and so nobody was angry at being told she wasn't.

It was true, however, that sometimes Seraphina Victorova, the head teacher, would shake her head and say to herself, "I think Tatjana acts too old, too responsible for her own good. I wish that just once she would giggle and be silly like the other girls."

She was to have her wish.

When the various Petrograd colonies were being brought into Vladivostok, Tatjana's group came on the third train, right behind the train carrying the group from Tyumen. Tatjana's group was all girls, the Tyumen group predominantly boys. Each had its own group loyalties and so they tended to stay apart on the station platform while waiting for transport to take them to temporary quarters on Second River.

Clutching little Gregorii firmly by the hand, Tatjana sat on a bench with several of her friends and watched the Tyumen boys romping, racing back and forth. What a bore boys were, she thought. So untidy, so noisy, so insensitive. She was glad there had been no boys at Petropavlovsk; they just ruined everything when they were around.

Out of the shoving, shouting mass of boys she unaccountably became aware of one. Perhaps she noticed him because he did not shove and shout, he walked with a friend and was deep in conversation. He looked to be about her age, though he was thirteen, a year older, and his coloring was not unlike hers. His face was slender, and rather handsome it occurred to her. She speculated on what he was talking about. This surprised her, for previously she had never had the slightest curiosity about boys' conversations.

On his second trip down the platform the boy looked directly at her and she dropped her eyes at once, but not quick enough. Suddenly the boy broke away from his friend, went to the edge of the platform and began to walk an imaginary tightrope. He balanced himself with delicate placing of feet and elaborate waving of arms.

She watched, dumbfounded. Now what would make him do that? A moment ago he had been acting in a sensible manner and now he was pretending to be some sort of circus performer. What would he do next? She watched to find out.

The boy was dangerously near the edge of the platform and suddenly his teacher, Nikolay Borsouk, shouted, "Peter! Stop that!"

The boy stopped, stiffened, his eyes went wide in horror. Then he clutched his chest, as if the words had been bullets and had penetrated to his heart. He began to stagger, his mouth gaping, his eyes working with the pain of it all. Several times he almost fell to his knees but with the greatest heroism remained erect.

Suddenly Tatjana giggled. The boy heard the giggle and he knew its source. Now his agony doubled. His knees trembled, his head rolled, his hands clawed at his chest. He fell to his knees, then on his side, then he flopped onto his back and his arms and legs went spread eagle in the rigidity of death.

Tatjana clapped her hand over her mouth but could not stifle the giggles that welled up hysterically.

Nikolay Borsouk stood over the boy and said firmly, "Peter Azaroff, have you lost your mind completely? Get on your feet and come along. The trucks have arrived to take us to the barracks."

Peter climbed to his feet and meekly followed the teacher without a glance in any direction. When he had gone Tatjana recovered her composure and was able to say, quite disdainfully, "What a silly, silly boy."

But for the first time in her life she dissembled. What she said to her secret self was, "What an amusing boy."

At this moment Seraphina Victorova came striding down the platform and clapped her hands above her head to attract attention. "All right, girls, the motor trucks have arrived. Pick up all your packages. Everyone . . . this way."

As they started to troop out of the station, the teacher fell into step with Tatjana and said, "What were you giggling about, dear?"

Gregorii was lagging, pulling on Tatjana's arm, so she bent down and hoisted him to her shoulder where he lay down his head and closed his eyes. Then Tatjana said, "Oh, nothing."

"Nothing?" the teacher repeated, a statement of her disbelief.

Tatjana did not repeat her denial, she merely walked along in silence, carrying her brother.

The teacher's feelings were wounded, for she had never before been rebuffed by Tatjana; the girl had always answered questions with open innocence. But this was a different girl. A boy clowning for her benefit had worked a profound and lasting change in her. She suddenly had a secret life and it contained only Peter Azaroff and herself. She looked down at the sleeping child but for the first time did not see Gregorii but rather her own arm encircling him. She caressed her own elbow and thought what a delightful elbow it was. When she arrived at the barracks she found a mirror, looked at herself and thought she had never seen a more winning smile than the one in the glass. She was beholding what Peter beheld, and she was thrilled and happy for both of them.

The *Yomei Maru,* Japanese freighter chartered by the American Red Cross for the desperate voyage around the world with 780 Petrograd children.

r. Rudolph Teusler, head of the nerican Red Cross Siberian Com- ssion.

Riley Allen, successor to Dr. Teusler in 1919, savior of the Wild Children of the Urals.

Relief officials board a train for an inspection trip of American hospitals deep in Siberia. Riley Allen is on the left. Burle Bramhall second from the right.

Barracks #7. American Red Cross headquarters in Vladivostok.

TWELVE

Now that the children were together on Russian Island, they stopped having adventures and settled down to growing. School was reestablished, and care was taken that it become an accredited institution so that the children might go on to higher classes after their return home. Special classes were organized for backward students, and special classes for those with talent for music or art.

The older boys were given chances to learn trades: carpentry, tailoring, cooking. About a dozen of the older girls were taken daily to the hospital in Vladivostok to become nurses' aides. A newspaper, *Bric-a-Brac,* was written, illustrated and published weekly by the students. There were dances every Saturday night, and once a month there were recitations and plays presented. The older boys from the Tyumen group put on Chekov's *Wedding* to great applause.

When the holidays came there were great festivities. Peter Azaroff recorded them in his diary: "We trimmed the tree and decorated the clubroom until 3 A.M. We had lots of trimmings for the tree and hung garlands and lamps in the study hall and the clubroom. We also hung a huge American flag and a smaller Russian one . . . When we woke up the next day the barracks looked very festive . . . For lunch we had goose with cabbage, and tea and jam. At 4 P.M. cocoa and jam. Our guests from Barracks No. 7 arrived after tea and the show started at 5 P.M.; musical numbers, poetry reading, singing . . . Presents were given to all the members of the colony after the show. Everybody got a toilet kit and a turkish towel, a piece of soap, a handkerchief and a knitted cap. Also a box of candy, nuts, an apple and a tangerine. Afterwards we had dinner and dancing until midnight. A buffet had been set up in the clubroom with tea, jam, cookies, nuts and tangerines. The dance was very gay. I danced several times with Tatjana Nikolenko. She dances very well."

Each week there was a staff meeting on the island during which Allen listened to the Russian teachers and tried to resolve whatever problems had developed. Food was a chronic problem, of course. The children's weekly consumption totaled 2,000 eggs, 2,000 pounds of meat, 1,600 pounds of fish, 1,400 pounds of flour, 1,600 pounds of cabbage and 1,600 pounds of onions. It was a formidable job to obtain such supplies in a city virtually under siege, but somehow it was done.

The larger problem showed no susceptibility to solution, however. Each week one of the Russians would ask when they could expect to return home to Petrograd. And each week Allen had to reply he just didn't know. The civil war was spreading and the Trans-Siberian Railway had been blown up so often and in so many places that it had all but ceased to be a railroad and was merely a long series of disjointed sections of track on which sat stalled and rusting equipment. Each week Allen renewed his pledge that the children would be returned to their parents at the earliest possible moment, but he could not guess when that moment would be.

"If the children could only write to their parents," one of the teachers said with a sigh. "It's been a year and a half since they left home and they need some contact."

"Let me look into that," Allen said.

The more he looked into it the more impossible it seemed. Without a completely functioning railroad there was just no way to send mail west. Then he reasoned, if not west why not east? Why not across the oceans? The distance was staggering; besides, Europe and the Baltics were not free of the various wars of liberation, the civil wars. There were hostile frontiers to be penetrated, suspicion and apathy to overcome. In an exhausted and disordered world who would care that a child had written a letter? Who would make an effort to send it on its way?

Undismayed, Allen bore in on the problem. He harassed the American consular officials until he finally got the creaking apparatus of diplomacy in motion—not much motion, but enough. It was arranged that mail from the children would be shipped across the Pacific to America, then across the Atlantic and through the North Sea into the Baltic and Stockholm. There it would be given to the Swedish government, which had remained neutral in the war, for shipment to the office of the International Red Cross in Tallinn, Estonia. From there it would be sent two hundred miles overland to Petrograd.

And it worked! Enough people cared to make it work!

Out of Russian Island in Vladivostok there now began a steady stream of letters full of good spirits and optimism. To parents, lost in the gloom of Petrograd, they must have been tonic.

❋ ❋ ❋ ❋ ❋

Mrs. V. M. Yacobson
Geslirovaky No. 5 Quarters No. 65
Petrograd

Dear Mamma: I am writing to you in a hurry because the letters must be turned in immediately. We all—God be praised—are sound and safe and are wishing for you. We are clothed and fed very well. All of us have three blankets, warm trousers, linen a.s.o. We are hoping to go soon to Petrograd. Also all of us are attending the higher Elementary school . . . I am in the fourth, Sergey is in the fifth and Kosta in the second class. We have here our own club, are making up dancing literary evenings and in general living very merry. We are kissing strongly very strongly you, Nadiu, and grandmother. Our greeting to our relatives and acquaintances. In the meantime good bye for the present. We shall see each other ere long.

Sergey, Kostia, Lidia Yacobson.

* * * * *

Alexandra Alexeivna Burmistrova
Tarasoff Pereulok House No. 26
Petrograd

I am greeting you my sweet and dear Mama. How do you do? How is your health? Sweet Mamma, we are sound and safe. We are living at Vladivostok on Russian Island under the auspices of the American Red Cross. We are living very well . . . We are all very satisfied. Dear Mamma, the Americans are very hospitable, kind and hard working. Dear Mamma, they want to transport us in May to Petrograd. Next Xmas we shall celebrate at home together with you. We are praying to God that He would help us to make all ready for our journey. God keep you safe. We are kissing you strongly. Liza and Lena Burmistrova.

* * * * *

Elizabeta Alexeyvna Teveethova
Oetrograd Corchovaia Street No. 34 quarters No. 49
Petrograd

Dear Mamma, grandmother, Misha, Katia, Verotshka and all others: I am greeting you. How do you do? We are all right . . . Americans are taking care of us. They teach us and furnish us with clothing and supply with food. Can you imagine that they are giving shelter to more than 600 children. Nobody has been offended . . . In the town arrived many soldiers but nobody knows who they are. Some people say that those are Bolsheviks. But it is so hard to believe all rumors, because many people are telling not always the truth. We enjoyed the holidays very cheerfully. Your daughter, Lidia Teveetkova.

One of the first children to receive an answer back from Petrograd was Peter Azaroff. His father wrote: "We were all very worried when we heard that the Red Cross had taken you . . . to Vladivostok. We know that we will not see you for a long time but we are happy because you write that you are well and not hungry as we all are here. It will be hard for you to believe that we spent 5,000 rubles a month to buy grain and dried herring; even then the quantity is so small that we are starving . . . Every month we lose more weight. Many of our friends have died. We're thus doubly thankful to know that you are in good hands, that you have enough to eat and nice warm clothes."

The exchange of letters could not have pleased the Soviets, for they revealed that the children were being well cared for by the Red Cross, whereas their parents, citizens of the "new order," were starving. But with a developing new Bolshevik technique of boldly calling black white and white black, a counterattack was all prepared.

That January, Red Cross Headquarters in Washington received a letter from the U.S. Department of State. The letter was forwarded to Riley Allen. It read:

Gentlemen: The Bolshevik wireless news sent out from Moscow on November 29, 1919, and intercepted in London, contains the following accusation against the American Red Cross: 'The People's Commissary for Education, Lunacharsky, publishes in IZVESTIA a telegram he has received reporting the fate of the former Petrograd Children's Colony, which was transferred from Petrograd in 1917 by the Union of Towns and was placed by Kolchak's Minister for Home Affairs under the uncontrolled administration of the American Red Cross. According to the statements of the priest of the village of Tagurovak and of the local inhabitants, the children lived under the most disgraceful conditions, both physically and morally. The children begged in the streets and implored the inhabitants to give them work, hoping to earn some means of existence. The Americans made the children work as assistants in their shops. In the end of May, just before the arrival of the Reds, the Americans removed the children to a destination unknown. Their departure took place at night. The children were given two hours to get ready. During their journey one small girl was drowned and many of the children contracted serious illnesses. At station Kurgan boys over 15 were mobilized. Lunacharsky adds that the cruel and senseless treatment of the children by the Americans should prove not only to the parents of the unfortunate captive children, but also to all those who are wavering in their political beliefs, what they may expect from the representatives of civilized imperialist Governments.

Then the State Department letter to the Red Cross concluded with:

As this Department believes it would perhaps be well to give the press a statement in this connection, it is thought that you would care to investigate the matter and furnish the truth concerning it.

When Allen read the letter at his staff meeting there was a moment of stunned silence, then an explosion of outrage and anger. He let the emotions run their course, then he added his own quiet words:

"It seems to me unwise to become engaged in any propaganda battle with the Bolsheviks. I shall report the facts of the Colony to Washington, of course, but I think that our best defense against this kind of attack is a firm restatement of our policy—that we shall care for these children only until they can be returned to their parents. And that we shall bend every effort to return them at the earliest date."

Allen subsequently sent a calm and balanced report to his superiors in Washington:

THE AMERICAN RED CROSS

Commission to Siberia

Vladivostok, Siberia
January 28th, 1920.

FROM: Acting Chairman, Executive Committee,
             Siberian Commission, Vladivostok

TO: Dr. Livingston Farrand, Chairman, Executive
        Committee, The American Red Cross

SUBJECT: *Return of Petrograd Children*

In your cable No. 1257 you ask for additional details about the children of Petrograd. Former correspondence about these children has acquainted you with the conditions under which their care was assumed by The American Red Cross and it is the opinion of the Commissioner and the Executive Committee of the Siberian Commission that the Red Cross cannot do less than return them to Petrograd, where most of their parents were living at the time they were sent across the Urals for safety.

The care of these children and the continuance of their education has been one of the most significant works the Red Cross has undertaken in Siberia and the fact that they are healthy and vigorous-looking, with a very small percentage of sickness, is commented on favorably by visitors of different nationalities seeing them.

The total number of these children in round numbers is eight hundred. There are teachers who have been with them all the time and whom we consider are part of the Colony. The total number of people to be returned will approximate eight hundred and thirty. Supervising, medical and nursing personnel make the total number for whom transportation must be secured eight (hundred) and fifty-five.

The situation politically seems to be clearing. Recent events give rise to the belief that within two months we will be able to send these children through to Petrograd. This does not take into consideration the physical condition of the Trans-Siberian Railway. If trains can be sent through, it will require about four trains, but up to this time we have not been able to get definite data about the cost of sending these children through. We estimate it would take four trains with sleeping, dining, kitchen and medical equipment to accommodate the children and the attendant personnel. Before we can offer a definite recommendation, it will be necessary to complete these estimates. As soon as these are secured we will cable you. . . .

R. H. Allen

RHA : HM

By the middle of February, Allen had completed the organization of the first train and it was standing in the Second River Station, waiting to take the children aboard. They never arrived, for again history frustrated the efforts to unite them with their parents.

It had become clear by now that the Allied intervention in Siberia was a shambles. Omsk had fallen to the Bolsheviks and their armies were advancing east of Lake Baikal. The British and French had already evacuated most of their forces and at the very moment Allen was trying to put his train together, the United States Secretary of State was preparing orders to General Graves that he withdraw all United States troops from the field into Vladivostok in preparation for complete evacuation.

Allen had foreseen these events. When he had written his superiors that "the situation politically seems to be clearing," he was stating an assumption that the Bolsheviks would soon be in control of all of the Trans-Siberian Railway and would allow him to return the children over it to Petrograd. What he did not foresee, nor did the American State Department, was the action of the Japanese.

The Japanese did not withdraw a single man from Siberia, and they looked upon the American, British and French actions with a smile that was far from inscrutable. By their withdrawal, the Allies were creating exactly what the Japanese had been hoping for, a power vacuum into which they could move and set up a puppet government.

Throughout the winter and early spring of 1920 the Japanese expanded their area of control until they were able to stop all movement of railroad traffic in and out of Vladivostok. The children could not be gotten out of the city without Japanese approval and assistance, which they were not about to give. And even if that had been possible, all track had been destroyed to the east of Chita. The Red Cross trains could have traveled, at best, one thousand miles and then would be stranded in land still ravaged by war and revolution.

What was the alternative? To sit tight until the railroad was repaired and controlled by a single power? But without the presence of American troops, would not the position of the Colony be precarious? The answer to this came quickly.

General Graves and his troops withdrew from Vladivostok on April 1, 1920. Just before dawn on the morning of April 4, Allen awoke to the sound of small arms fire that seemed to come from a dozen different places throughout the city. He rolled out of bed to meet Bramhall coming down the corridor.

Bramhall shouted, "The Japanese are taking over the city."

Together they looked out a window on the third floor to see that the Japanese flag had been run up on all the public and government buildings. While they stared, an errant bullet smashed the window and embedded itself in the wall behind their heads.

"Get to the women's dorm," Allen ordered, "and tell Mother Campbell to keep the girls down low. No one is to leave the compound."

Bramhall took off on a run, but he found that Mother Campbell already had everyone lying on the floor.

"We're all right here," she reported briskly. "I've got a half-dozen older Colony girls in my room, nurses' aides, but they're fine. Just tell me what's happening."

"The Japanese are taking over the city."

"Our nurses had better get to the hospital."

"Not until the shooting around here ends. Not until Riley gives the order."

"Thank God most of the children are on Russian Island, safe from all this."

"Let's hope," Bramhall said grimly.

As they talked there came a great commotion from the direction of the main gate in the wall surrounding the compound. There was a standing order that it be locked every night, and now a man was shaking it hysterically and begging to be let in. He was a Korean, one of a dozen employed by the Red Cross. He was admitted and he ran to Allen where he dropped on his knees and babbled an all but incoherent story. It was finally clear that all of his Korean friends had been arrested by the Japanese and were going to be shot. He begged that the Red Cross save them.

Allen considered the problem for several moments. This was perhaps the right place to take a stand against the Japanese. What he feared from them was not a move against his own people—their Red Cross Uniforms would probably protect them—but against the children. This had to be forestalled at all costs, so he told the Korean that he would immediately protest to the Japanese about his countrymen, demand that they be freed.

By the time Allen got dressed and drove out of the compound, the shooting had ceased and the Japanese were in full control of the city. Everywhere the sons of Nippon were marching, strutting, grinning, waving their rifles in triumph. As he drove down the main street he came upon groups of Russian prisoners being herded along by Japanese bayonets.

Allen went directly to the office of the Japanese Civilian Commissioner, Matsu Daria. He was a gentle and cultured man with whom Allen had had pleasant relations in the past. There was some question about what control he had over the military, but Allen chose at this time to assume it was complete.

"Mr. Commissioner," Allen said, "it is reported to me that the Imperial Japanese Army has arrested a dozen Koreans who are employees of the American Red Cross. This is a most serious development and might have far-reaching consequences. You must understand, sir, that these Koreans are under our protection. Unless there are specific charges against them, I must demand their immediate release."

Matsu Daria pursed his lips, then said softly, "I will investigate."

"Personally," Allen said firmly.

Matsu Daria nodded. "Personally."

The Koreans were released the next day and returned happily to work for the Red Cross, which they considered the most powerful organization on earth.

Allen was not misled by this easy victory. He knew that once the Japanese militarists had consolidated their power they would not be so ready to bow to civilian demands for moderation. The days of Matsu Daria's influence were numbered, and when they ran out, nothing would be safe from the whims and the appetites of the military. A colony of Russian children would be a prize of first rank, if only for their value as hostages.

Upon returning to Barracks No. 7 Allen called a meeting of his staff to discuss the looming crisis. He reported the situation as he saw it, ending with, "At all costs we must keep the children out of Japanese hands."

"That may not be easy," Bramhall observed, "with American troops gone."

"Quite right," Allen said briskly. "Our position in Vladivostok is untenable. We'll have to move the Colony someplace else."

"Move the Colony!" several voices echoed in disbelief. "To where?"

Allen unrolled a map and spread it on the table. "Let's find out."

Over the next hour they examined and discarded a half-dozen areas in the Maritime Provinces, in Manchuria, in Korea. It seemed impossible to find a spot that was beyond Japanese influence and still safe from the fighting fronts. But even if such a place could be found, all plans foundered upon one insurmountable obstacle—the Japanese controlled all the railroad traffic in and out of Vladivostok. Not a bale of hay could be moved without their permission, and they would most certainly not cooperate in the escape of the Colony. They were trapped.

After the talk had run out, Allen sat brooding over the map. "Riley," one of his staff said gently, "we've done all we can for the children."

Allen raised his eyes to look at the speaker. "Have we?" he said. There was an edge to his voice, a steeliness that no one had ever before heard. This man of gentle persuasion had altered. The pressure of events had not softened him but fused him to new hardness. And if all the logic of the situation was against him, he would simply stop being logical, he would substitute a fierce stubbornness. Whatever else, he would not surrender.

The staff sat silent and slightly ill at ease. After several moments he said, quite matter-of-factly, "Since we're cut off by land, there is only one thing for us to do. We'll put to sea."

THIRTEEN

The decision to go to sea resolved one problem but created many new ones. Once the Colony was afloat it could not just drift, chartless and rudderless, it would have to go someplace. Where? Why not right to Petrograd?

The bold idea produced some problems of logistics. Such a voyage would mean almost circling the globe and not every ship could quarter and feed eight hundred children on such an odyssey.

Sailing in the nearby Sea of Japan were a number of large passenger ships owned by White Russians, and Allen opened negotiations to charter one of them. When the owners discovered that the ship would be used to return the children to the "murderous Bolsheviks," they broke off all talks.

With no other ships in the area adequate to the job, Allen turned to America for help. The war was over and there were still thousands of tons of shipping being operated by the Army Transport Command, the War Shipping Board, the Navy, and, of course, the various private lines. These vessels were being dispatched around the world to bring home troops, supplies, return prisoners of war to their homelands, and perform various other postwar housekeeping jobs. Allen wanted one ship for two months. Incredibly, he was turned down. The War Department, which had the authority to assign him a ship, was not moved by his plea on behalf of the children.

At this moment the Bolsheviks stepped up their propaganda offensive and released to the world press a statement purportedly signed by the Petrograd Parents Committee that demanded the immediate return of the children. They did not suggest just how it was to be done. Then, cruelly, the Reds cut the line of communication between parents and children; no more mail was allowed to pass between them. Allen must have sometimes felt that he and his small staff were alone in a hostile or forgetful world. He watched the Bay of the Golden Horn with some bitterness during the month of May as it became full of Allied transport to take out the Czechs but not one vessel to rescue his children.

He inundated the Washington Headquarters with requests for help; he wrote old friends who might be in a position of influence, and among them was Dr. Teusler who had returned to Japan. And then, at the end of May, a ship available for charter was found. She was called the *Yomei Maru*, and she was a ten-thousand-ton deadweight freighter owned by the Katsuda Steamship Company of Japan. She had just made her maiden voyage at a cruising speed of ten knots. Her captain was N. Kayahara, and under him served sixty-seven officers and crew. She might not be perfect for the job but she was available and Allen took her. He was to find too late how *im*perfect she was.

In his letter to Washington on June 7, Allen reported the chartering of the *Yomei Maru* and made a few comments about the War Department. His language was restrained, but revealing of his emotions on the subject:

THE AMERICAN RED CROSS
Commission to Siberia

Vladivostok, Siberia
June 7th, 1920

Mr. F. P. Keppel,
Vice-Chairman, Executive Committee
A.R.C. National Headquarters
Washington, D.C., USA

Dear Mr. Keppel:

We have signed the charter for the "Yomei Maru" to take the children to Petrograd and we expect to get them off the latter part of this month.

From our experience with the various people who claim to be officials of the Russian Volunteer Fleet, we are convinced that we should have nothing to do with the boats of that fleet. Notwithstanding the good intentions and desires of the Russian Ambassadors at Washington and perhaps in other places, one cannot safely use the boats of that fleet. There are too many groups claiming control and exercising some control. The captains of some of the ships seem to be acting upon their own initiative and pay no attention to orders of any of the groups who contend they control things.

I think we would make a serious mistake if we put any freight or passengers on any of these boats.

The Czechs have many tons of freight in excess of the boats which have been chartered by them or which are to be sent for their use. It is, therefore, absolutely impossible to get any help from them. It will be many months before they get all their freight away.

We are exceedingly sorry that our War Department could not be induced to furnish us a boat to take the children home. Aside from the Red Cross, I think it would have been good advertising for both the War Department and the State Department.

No-one in the States who has not been here, and especially during the recent weeks, can appreciate the antipathy of the Russians toward the Japanese and everything Japanese. It was only after we had exhausted every other resource that the local Russian authorities expressed any willingness to have the children taken away in a Japanese boat.

Again I express the regret that the War Department was not able to help us. When we hear of the frequency with which transports are diverted from one purpose to another, it makes me feel that that department might have assisted us in this case. . . .

R. H. Allen

With their destinies tied to the *Yomei Maru,* Allen and his staff took a hard look at the ship and the problems she presented. They were considerable. She was a dry-cargo freighter with quarters on deck for her crew, and no one else. To put aboard her eight hundred children plus their teachers and the Red Cross staff, to feed them and sleep them and wash their clothes and tend their sicknesses . . . how was it to be done? They would simply have to be packed below decks where the cargo ordinarily went. But in the cargo holds there were no portholes, no ventilation, no lights, no plumbing . . . nothing but the hard bulkheads of riveted steel. To place human beings in such iron cages for a ten-knot voyage almost around the world seemed to promise disaster. The only thing that seemed worse was the alternative—staying in Vladivostok.

There was no time for structural changes in the *Yomei Maru,* it would have to be makeshift. Allen sent his engineering officer, Ward Walker, to Japan to supervise the refitting of the ship, instructing him to bring her to Vladivostok no later than the first week in June.

Allen had already decided that he would personally sail with the *Yomei Maru.* He was determined to see the job to the end, and he began the delicate and vital work of picking his staff. He knew at once that he wanted Bramhall as business manager. If ever this lanky, laconic man's efficiency was needed, it would be on this voyage. Nor could Allen conceive of successfully controlling, teaching, and diverting the children without Mother Campbell's loving heart and unquenchable optimism. Since her husband had a job in Shanghai and could take their two children there to await her return, she accepted the assignment. The rest of the staff was also selected because they had done outstanding work in Siberia. And every man and woman was eager to serve aboard ship. They were, besides Allen, Bramhall and Campbell:

Chief surgeon, Dr. H. O. Eversole, Los Angeles, California; finance officer, Clarence Rowland, Buffalo, New York; quartermaster, F. A. Delgado, Jacksonville, Florida; chief steward,

W. P. Ambrose, Baltimore, Maryland; engineer officer, Ward
Walker, Maui, Hawaii; chief nurse, Miss Florence Farmer, On-
tario, Canada; physicians, Dr. H. M. Davison, Greensboro,
Georgia; Dr. W. T. Barger, Cleveland, Ohio; Dr. C. H. Gano,
Pittsburgh, Pennsylvania; Dr. H. M. Coulter, Pasadena, California; stenographer, Miss Stacy M. Snow, Seattle, Washington; recreation officer, Henry C. Woods, YMCA, Siberia.

And from the former prisoners of war they chose men and
women with the skills essential to a self-contained community:
shoemakers, tailors, cooks and waiters, electricians and plumbers. Seventy-seven men were chosen, all of whom had previously worked for the Red Cross in one capacity or another.
There were Hungarians, Austrians, Czechs, Slovaks, Poles,
Germans and Letts. And for each man chosen, there were a
dozen who begged to be taken. They wanted to go for a variety of reasons, some for adventure, most for escape from the
bleak land of Siberia. That this voyage might turn into a
nightmare was something they didn't consider. Or if they did,
a floating nightmare seemed no worse than the landlocked one
they had been living.

Financing for the voyage was now undertaken by Fred Winfrey, controller of the Siberian Commission. His figures revealed that the charter hire, at $4,500 per day, would run to an
estimated total of $315,000; alterations to the boat, $100,000;
coal, $115,000; food, $75,000; salaries, equipment and return of
A.R.C. personnel, $75,000. The salary item included $12 a
month paid to the P.O.W.'s and the Russian teachers, and
spending money for the children which ranged from fifty cents
to $1.50 a month depending upon age. The projected total
came to $680,000. It a was staggering obligation for the Red
Cross to take on, but Washington headquarters never questioned the moral commitment or the cost.

Actually, Winfrey's figures turned out to be low. But he
could not have foreseen the strange odyssey for which the
Yomei Maru was fated.

Keeping track of the children during transfer from Russian

Island to the ship, and during shore leaves in the various ports they might hit, would be a difficult job, but Bramhall came up with a plan that was simplicity itself. He gave every child a number. He had aluminum tags struck off with the child's number on it to be worn on a thong around the neck at all times. The children were to board the ship and debark in numerical sequence, their numbers being checked at the gangplank. Thus, if number 48 followed 46 it would be immediately apparent that number 47 was missing. This required a final and complete human inventory on Russian Island. The result was:

Number of boys	428	
Number of girls	352	
Children		780
American personnel:		
Male	13	
Female	4	
	17	
Russian personnel:		
Male	10	
Female	75	
	85	
Other personnel (P.O.W.'s)	78	
Personnel		180
Total		960

The average age of the boys and girls was between twelve and thirteen. The oldest child in the Colony was twenty, and the youngest, three. Nationalities other than Russian were: fifteen Polish children, eight Letts, five Estonians, two French, and one each Lithuanian, Finnish, Persian, Swiss and English.

The *Yomei Maru* sailed into the Bay of the Golden Horn on the afternoon of July 9, and all the Americans stood on the quay behind their compound, straining to get the first glimpse of her. She came in slowly, riding high. She looked like a "Hog

Islander," a ship mass-produced in America during the war without benefit of a good marine architect. She was a "T-square" boat, made flat with no camber to the deck and no sheer fore and aft. This meant that the water would inevitably stand in puddles on the deck and not drain off into the scuppers. Her single stack was thin and straight, without rake. She had an unlovely silhouette.

What did look fine were the enormous letters on her sides which read "American Red Cross," and the shining red cross painted on her stack. These gave purpose to the ship, they gave her gallantry. One could not look at her without being moved.

When Allen went aboard he found that Ward Walker had achieved a masterpiece of improvisation. On deck there were five great hatches leading down to the cargo holds. The bottommost hold under each hatch was to carry a cargo of five thousand tons of sugar from Vladivostok to New York, which would help pay the cost of the expedition. The between deck holds were where the children would be berthed. Steel cots were held in triple tiers in two-by-four wooden frames. Ventilation was most important, and Ward had rigged a canvas wind sail over each hatch. The sail scooped the wind into a big canvas tube about four feet in diameter and the tube carried the fresh air down to the hold. Stale air was to be expelled by two large electric fans rigged amidships to face another set of canvas tubes that ran back up out of the hatches to leeward.

A series of latrines and showers had been constructed on deck, starboard for the boys and portside for the girls. A completely equipped hospital area had been constructed, with operating room, twenty-four beds in a general ward and twenty-four beds in an isolation ward. On the bridge deck, temporary cabins had been constructed for the Red Cross staff. On the starboard afterdeck was the galley, constructed in such a manner that the whole thing could be pushed overboard in case of fire.

And with disquieting foresight, Walker had constructed a

brig on the poopdeck. It was made of two-by-fours, laid up together like a log cabin in the Old West. High up was a series of windows for ventilation, too small for a child to escape. The door was of heavy planking with massive iron hinges and a great padlock.

As Walker took Allen and the rest of the Red Cross personnel on a tour of the ship, Captain Kayahara remained aloof in his cabin. Allen puzzled about this and decided that protocol must not have been properly observed. The captain had obviously expected Allen to present himself when first boarding the ship, and not having done so, the captain could not now seek him out.

"What sort of man is the captain?" Allen asked Walker.

Walker shrugged his shoulders. "Knows his job. He doesn't speak English and so we didn't get very chummy."

"I think you'd better take me up to his cabin so I can meet him."

If Captain Kayahara was offended, there was no way of telling it from his impassive face as he received Allen. He bowed formally and offered his guest a chair and ordered tea served. His first officer spoke English and was present to translate.

After the amenities had been disposed of, Allen came to the point. "Captain Kayahara, I'm certain we will have a good voyage. I am aware of your reputation as an excellent seaman and officer, and I deem it a privilege to sail with you. Though this ship is in charter to the American Red Cross, and to me as its representative, I recognize your authority as absolute insofar as the operation of the ship is concerned. However, I am in charge of the Colony. I shall determine all duties and discipline of the children, their teachers, the prisoners of war, and my own Red Cross staff. Is that understood and agreeable?"

The captain listened to the translation, then nodded that he understood and it was agreed.

As the day of embarkation approached, a variety of problems pressed for attention. There were twelve children suffering from malnutrition who would require special diets. There were fourteen mentally defective children who would require special supervision. And there were eight invalids who would have to be put immediately in sick bay. The invalids included a boy with a post hyphemic condition (bleeding in the eyes that might produce blindness); a girl with chronic endocarditis (heart inflammation that might result in death); a boy with dermatitis herpetiformis (chronic skin infection with open lesions); a girl with vomitus nervosus (constant vomiting and therefore slow starvation); a girl with hysteria and epilepsy; and a girl and a boy with dementia praecox (schizophrenia—potential suicides).

It was fortunate that out of 780 children there were but 34 who could be considered a health problem. Yet these cases, handled so matter-of-factly on land, would assume greater weight and concern when confined to a ship at sea. The *Yomei Maru* would squeeze and concentrate all human qualities, both good and bad.

There was a final statistic that was of some significance: almost fifty percent of the children were in or approaching adolescence.

Shortly before noon on July 12 three tugboats, squat and fussy as hens, began to herd a half-dozen dry-cargo barges across the Bay of the Golden Horn. Packed aboard the barges were the children and teachers of the Petrograd Colony and they were being taken to the side of the *Yomei Maru*. As each child climbed the gangplank and dropped on deck, he spoke his number and was immediately sent below to his designated bunk. They were divided according to sex; the girls in the forward holds No. 1 and No. 2, the boys in the after holds No. 5 and No. 6. There were a few exceptions. Tatjana Nikolenko requested that her little brother Gregorii be allowed to live in the bunk beneath hers. This was permitted.

On this day Riley Allen made his first entry in the ship's log:

"American flag run up on the *Yomei Maru* for the first time at 10:00 A.M. During the day a number of visitors came aboard the ship, including General Cecek, Commander of the Czech Forces, and representatives of the City and Provincial Governments. The Russian Island Colony arrived . . . on barges just before noon . . . sent over early in the afternoon for hospital patients . . . all visitors ashore at 8 P.M. . . . With a triple check on the lists of children, we feel certain that we have embarked every child of the Colony. Teachers and educators of each group report that their entire personnel is aboard . . . Twelve o'clock midnight made final trip ashore, sending cable to Washington and to Commissioner at Tokyo that we were sailing at daylight next day."

The log, Tuesday, July 13, 1920: "4 A.M.; after loading cargo all night and finishing about 3 A.M. ship's hatches were covered, and ship getting ready for sea. The Captain has had steam up since the previous day. At 4 o'clock Captain Kayahara asked me if we were ready to leave and I gave the order to go at 4:30 A.M. . . . started down the bay at 4:32 A.M. Foggy weather. Children and personnel soon appeared on deck, saying farewell to Vladivostok . . ."

The morning of July 14 dawned with a smooth sea, no wind and flashes of sunshine between cumulus clouds. At 5:30 A.M. the first bell rang throughout the *Yomei Maru* and it began to buzz with voices like a great, floating beehive.

First mess call was at seven, and under Mother Campbell's direction the P.O.W.'s assigned to the galley carried kettles of cereal to the mess tables set midship under canvas awnings. The younger children ate first, the older ones next, the adults last. The Red Cross was an old hand at organizing things, and each hour of this coming day was allocated to some activity. At nine, there would be a general inspection of quarters by Bramhall and Walker to see that the beds had been made, the decks swept. At 10:30 A.M. school would convene. The subjects to be studied were algebra, geometry, physics, arithmetic, Russian, English, French, German, history, geography, and natural history.

At twelve-thirty the first dinner call was scheduled, and at three afternoon school would begin. Afternoon inspection was to be at four-thirty and then the deck would be cleared for drills and exercises and games and sports. Supper was scheduled for six, with lights out at nine-thirty, except on Saturday nights when the bedtime was advanced to eleven to allow for entertainment and dancing.

Lifeboat drills would be daily but at different hours. During such drills each child would don a life jacket and report to his station. The boys were assigned to the twenty-three rafts, the girls to the twelve boats, all of which had been stocked with emergency rations.

It was also arranged that part of the work aboard ship would be done by the children. Some of the larger boys were assigned to duty as dining-room stewards, others to handling the food stores. The older girls who had already received nurses' aide training in Vladivostok were assigned to the infirmary. Other girls would be expected to assist in the linen room and the laundry. The Boy Scouts and Girl Scouts were to become orderlies assigned to the executive office. Even the smaller children would have their turn of duty as *dejournies* in which they served their own mess table and cleaned up the dishes afterward.

It was a program well thought out, based upon years of experience. The only trouble was that in all those years the Red Cross had never had the experience of mothering eight hundred children aboard a Japanese freighter.

FOURTEEN

Gregorii Nikolenko had the bottom bunk, his sister Tatjana the one above him, and another girl was above her. His bunk was very cozy and he was hardly aware of the fact that there were almost two hundred bunks just like his in the same dark hold. His straw-filled tick gave off fine crackling noises when he moved, and he could lay his ear against the mattress and then wiggle his feet or his hands and make the crackling at a distance or nearby.

His bunk, being close to the deck, allowed him to explore another phenomenon. He put a small hand down to touch the steel plates and found that they vibrated. He had never slept on a floor that jiggled in this manner. He put a naked foot over the side of his bunk to touch the floor, and received the same sensation.

"Gregorii!" his sister hissed at him from above. "Lie still and go to sleep."

He lay still and thought for a minute. *She* wasn't going to sleep. She was talking with the girl above her. All the girls were talking. He was in a black grotto full of cascading girlish voices; they swirled and eddied and, from time to time, sparkled with a shower of giggles. But *he* had been told to go to sleep.

There came to him at this moment something entirely new—a sense of justice. Or in this case, a sense of injustice. Gregorii was about to be five. Over the past year he had felt only the most impersonal emotions about people. Nine-tenths of his waking hours had been spent within his own mind, conducting games with inanimate objects as his playmates. He didn't feel strongly toward his sister and her friends, or toward the teachers or the Red Cross people because they existed in only the most distant and shadowy manner. But now, as his fifth birthday approached, he was suddenly joining them, becoming part of their world. Or perhaps, more accurately, they were becoming a part of his world. They were not always a welcome part, but they had arrived to stay.

His sister had observed many changes in him. He no longer allowed himself to be carried, nor did he walk—he was constantly running, hopping, skipping, jumping. Where he had been docile he was now assertive, bossy, boastful. He talked constantly, his words outrunning his knowledge. But he seemed determined to repair that lag, and his monologues were punctuated with the question "Why?"

Why was the moon white? Why did the wind blow? What made the floor jiggle? Why did Miss Zoren have hair on her lip?

Tatjana was dismayed at the outpouring of questions. To begin with, she didn't know the answers to many of them, but even when she was able to come up with an explanation, Gregorii was barely able to listen, so consumed was he with eagerness to formulate his next question. Nor would the most complete answers have really satisfied him, for he wanted to explore and touch and learn for himself.

His new strength and dexterity resulted in his being forever plucked from precarious places; in the rigging, on the rail, on the ladder leading to the engine room, on the lip of the deep tank where the meat was stored. Each time he was returned to

hold No. 2 kicking and squirming with outrage and frustration, he announced plans for dire vengeance. It seemed to him
that all the adults, including his sister, were engaged in a
conspiracy to keep him from seeing the wonderful curiousness
of things.

It was not just Gregorii who found the ship mysterious and
fascinating, but every child aboard. None of them had been at
sea before and there was not a corner of the Yomei Maru that
they did not penetrate, or attempt to. Discipline, which had
been so well established back at Russian Island, seemed to
disappear the moment they put to sea. Allen had foreseen this
and called a staff meeting on the first morning to discuss the
problem. Gathered in his small cabin, which had been constructed on the boat deck, were Eversole, chief surgeon;
Bramhall, business manager; Florence Farmer, chief nurse;
and Stacy Snow, the Commission secretary. They were waiting
for Mother Campbell when they heard her agitated voice in the
distance.

"Stop that! Come down here this minute! Stop . . . stop!
Do you hear me?"

Riley Allen walked around to starboard and found Mother
Campbell, her arms akimbo, her face flushed. He grinned at
her and said, "Trouble?"

"Look!" she cried.

A half-dozen of the older boys had placed some bentwood
chairs on the railing and were now seated atop them, teetering
back and forth. Behind them was a sheer drop into the sea.

"The chairs won't break, Mother Campbell," they called
back. "They're very strong."

"Your heads will break if you don't do what I say!"

It was a throat-catching moment while they climbed teeter-
ingly off the chairs onto the rail and finally dropped safely to
the deck. They placed the chairs in front of her with grins of
triumph. She turned to gesture toward the deckhouse, against
which were stacked four or five more chairs.

"A friend of mine gave them to me just before we sailed,"

she said to Allen. "I figured we could sit on them after dark and enjoy the stars. But I'm afraid they'll cause trouble. Not only will there be arguments over who sits on them, but in bad weather they'll bang around the deck, and there's sure no room to take them below. Riley, I'm gonna throw them overboard."

"They're your chairs," he grinned.

She told the boys to pitch them over the side. For a moment they couldn't believe their good fortune, but when they saw that she was serious, they let out a happy whoop and fell to. The chairs sailed over the side in a long, graceful arc, fell into the sea with a satisfying splash and for a moment disappeared from sight. Then one by one they came to the surface, righted themselves and rode along with their wooden seats just awash. Soon all ten chairs were clustered together on the surface, bobbing gently from time to time, looking like some ghostly marine conference engaged in an animated discussion. Slowly they disappeared astern, but not until a hundred or so children had boiled up out of the holds to watch the interesting performance.

The staff meeting finally convened and Dr. Eversole began to make his report. There were thirty-three dispensary cases, none serious enough for confinement; eight cases of scabies in the isolation ward; no seasickness and no contagious disease. At this point there came the sound of running feet on the deck and whoops of excitement. Allen looked at Mother Campbell, she looked briefly heavenward and then stepped out on deck.

Upon her appearance a bunch of girls shouted, "Mother Campbell . . . come and see!"

"Come and see what?" she demanded.

"In the washroom . . . the water lights up! Just as if there is electricity in it."

"Nonsense!" she snorted.

"It does! It does!" chorused the children.

From behind her came Allen's dry voice. "Better investigate, Mother Campbell."

She allowed herself to be swept aft by the waves of children.

Five minutes later she reappeared in the doorway of Allen's cabin and on her face was apologetic disbelief. "Riley . . ." She shook her head and started the sentence once more. "Riley . . . the water lights up. Don't grin at me, just come and see for yourself."

Again the staff meeting was disrupted and they all followed Mother Campbell toward the port side washrooms. Allen picked up Ward Walker on the way and explained their mission.

"Ha!" said Walker.

They found the washroom jammed with excited children and it took some minutes to shoo them out on deck. Then Allen took firm hold of a faucet and turned it on. The water came rushing out and it was undeniably luminous. It cast a cool white light that lit up the bowl, making it look like a full moon on a cloudless night. The adults stood in a mute circle. Allen turned off the water and the light was extinguished. He turned it on again and the bowl glowed with what seemed to be liquid electricity.

With a grunt, Ward Walker thrust a glass under the faucet, filled it with water and took it out on deck to squint at it. "Look here," he said to Allen, "it's full of marine life. There's something tiny in there, no bigger than pinpoints, millions of them, and they're phosphorescent. They glow like lightning bugs in a backyard."

"How did they get in our drinking water?" Bramhall demanded.

Walker didn't answer at once. He walked back into the washroom, turned on one of the showers. It did not glow. He cupped his hands under it and then tasted the water. "Damn!" he said.

"What is it, Ward?" Allen demanded.

The square-faced engineer sighed heavily and said, "The fresh tank is tied into the sea water system and the sea water comes out the fresh water pipes. I checked the fresh tank this morning and it had gone down alarmingly. I couldn't understand it, until now. The drinking water is being used for showers and washing dishes and scrubbing the clothes and cleaning the decks."

"How long will it last?"

"Two days, or three at the most."

"There are some plumbers among the P.O.W.'s," Riley said. "Can you find the trouble and have them fix it?"

"Much of the piping goes between the bulkheads. I don't know. I'll try to trace down the trouble right away."

All the rest of that morning and during the afternoon Walker was crawling over the ship, trying to trace the intricate network of pipes. A single wrong coupling, a T or an elbow, could cause the trouble, but where was it in all the miles of piping?

Before the trouble could be located, another crisis came to Riley Allen. This time it was Dr. Eversole who brought it. He said, "Riley, the toilets are backing up."

This was very bad news. An outbreak of contagious disease aboard a crowded ship was horrible to contemplate and to avoid it the most meticulous sanitation had to be observed.

"Let's have a look," Allen snapped.

A long line of toilets had been installed on both the starboard and port sides of the well deck. They flushed with water and emptied into a wooden trough that slanted downward toward the bow and ended in a vent that drained over the side. Allen and Eversole now found the trouble. An uneven loading of cargo had brought the stern of the ship lower than the bow and the troughs beneath the toilets were tilted backward instead of forward and would not gravity drain to the vent. The refuse had filled the troughs and was now overflowing onto the deck.

"If we had enough buckets we could have everyone use them and then throw the refuse over the side," Eversole volunteered.

"Did you ever try it in a high wind?" Allen asked him.

Eversole rubbed his chin and answered soberly, "No."

"The result can sometimes be spectacular," Allen said over his shoulder as he marched up to the bridge to consult with the captain. He asked what their next port of call would be. It was Muroran on the Japanese island of Hokkaido. When would they arrive? About noon on July 15. Allen instructed the captain to radio ahead, requesting that plumbers and carpenters meet the *Yomei Maru* on arrival.

In Muroran twoscore Japanese workmen swarmed aboard the ship and began the job of fixing the plumbing and the drainage. The children were given an afternoon ashore. Allen entered in the ship's log: ". . . The police asked us to form the children into columns of two and we marched this way through the town of Muroran to the Boys' Elementary School, where for an hour the Russian children saw the Japanese children in gymnastics and judo. It was an impressive sight when our children—about 650—went ashore, the others remaining on the ship at their own preference—lined up in the courtyard of the school with the dark-eyed, darkskinned and coal-black-haired Japanese ringed solid all around the Russians, most of whom are fair-haired and blue- or grey-eyed. From the boys' school we went to the Girls' Elementary School, where again the contrast was striking. The girls of the school sang a number of songs and then our girls responded with one of the Russian songs they know so well and sing so beautifully."

The *Yomei Maru* headed out of Muroran and into the Pacific at 1 P.M., July 16. Allen entered in the log:

"A trial was made of the water circulating system before leaving Muroran. The joints and fittings put in at Muroran leaked considerably, but it appears we shall be able to get sufficient sea water for all the bathing necessary and thus conserve fresh water. In addition to the defects in the water circulating system, a great number of small pieces of work aboard the ship has been badly done, for instance: The handles and locks on the doors leading to the washrooms and toilets are very flimsy and work very badly indeed. The handles began coming off the first day. The deck flooring is crude. There are large holes in it and it is not watertight at all. Dirt and various refuse easily collect underneath the planks and holes and through the cracks left by the shrinkage of the green boards.

"We are also having difficulty with the lighting system. It seems impossible to have all the hatches lighted at the same time, especially hatch No. 2 on the side occupied by the larger girls is often in total darkness. In this hatch the beds are three tiers deep and it is the largest hatch in the ship and should be well lighted throughout."

The absence of light in hold No. 2 was to have a dire result before the end of many days.

Hannah Campbell and her own children. She became "Mother" Campbell to all homesick Americans who lived in Barracks #7, Vladivostok.

arl Myers, American Red Cross
ld director in charge of the first
scue train that penetrated the
ttle lines to rescue the "wild
ildren" in the Ural Mountains.

Major General William S. Graves, commander of American armed forces in Siberia, 1919-1920.

Admiral Aleksandr Kolchak, commander of Siberian White Russian forces, visits Red Cross Hospital in Omsk, August, 1919. Kolchak is center with hand on sword; civilian to his left is U.S. Consul General E. L. Harris.

FIFTEEN

At the beginning of the voyage the weather was perfect. The days were sunwashed, the sea was calm, there was a following breeze. Body heat, plus heat from the engine room below, sent the temperature in the holds into the low 80's, which made their occupancy uncomfortable but not intolerable.

The children were brought on deck in groups, about a hundred at a time, for purposes of eating, studying and exercising. It became immediately clear, however, that the rather formalized program of calisthenics was insufficient to work off the pure animal energy that their small bodies generated. Henry Woods, the physical training director, organized wrestling matches between the older boys, and the younger children he simply ran round and round the deck until they were so sufficiently relaxed that they would stay in their bunks and study their lessons.

Finding running space on the *Yomei Maru* was not so simple, however. Much of the deck was cluttered with temporary structures such as galleys and toilets and living quarters for the Red Cross staff, and a good part of the remaining free space was piled with coal. The ship, overloaded as she was, could not make the full width of the Pacific with the fuel in her regular bunkers and she had to carry additional coal on deck. And on this cluttered deck the sailors had to move about and do the ship's work.

All of which presented to the children not a flat race course but all the excitement of an obstacle course, and they met the challenge with glad cries. The crew, however, began to raise strong objections, claiming that the races interfered with their work. The captain supported his men and stated their case to Allen. This problem was rather easily solved. The children would run on only one side of the ship, alternating daily between port and starboard. This seemed to satisfy all concerned.

On the night of July 16 the girls' chorus gave a concert on deck. The ship glided smoothly through a moonstruck sea, leaving a wake of silver bubbles. A hundred girls gathered in a huge semicircle amidships and raised their thin, sweet voices in ancient Russian songs. Even without understanding the words, one could tell that these songs told of Mother Earth, the love of home and fireside. The songs were darkly textured, rich with human longing and need. And coming now from the voices of these children adrift on a great ocean, the innocent victims of war and revolution, they were deeply moving.

The children in the audience sat quite still, the Americans were held in rapt attention, here and there a Russian teacher softly wept. The prisoners of war stared distantly at the sea and thought of their own homelands and their own families. Even the Japanese crew stopped work and turned contemplative faces toward the singers. The entire ship was caught in a common emotion of gentle sadness. And when the last haunting note had been raised and drifted off over the sea, all the children went down into the holds and to bed.

The ship was quiet except for the sibilance of water at bow and stern. A glow of a cigarette marked the darkness where Riley Allen leaned against a railing and looked seaward, lost in thought. A stocky figure moved along the deck toward him and then stopped a few feet away, awaiting his attention. The figure was that of Ward Walker. He was a practical man, a no-nonsense man, and he had probably been the least touched by the prevailing mood of the ship. It was obvious that he had come to report something; and it was equally obvious that Riley Allen was reluctant to break the mood of the night.

But finally, with a slight sigh, he turned and said, "Yes, Ward?"

"During the concert the lifeboats were pilfered," Walker said.

"And what was taken?"

"The emergency food rations."

"Hmmmm." Allen flipped his cigarette and made a glowing arc into the black waters below. "Any ideas about who did it?"

"Some of the children, of course."

"Why do you say 'of course'?"

"All the adults understand how essential that food would be if we had to take to the lifeboats. It could mean life or death. An adult thief might steal from the galley, from the cargo, but not from the lifeboats."

"You're probably right. Tomorrow morning during inspection I want you and Burle to make a thorough search of the bunks and find where the food is hidden, then bring those children to my cabin."

The next morning six boys stood before Allen. They ranged in age from eight to twelve years old; they ranged in attitude from defiance to contrition. One of them, twelve-year-old Boris Setkov, was obviously the leader and on his face there was only blandness. He had already set up his defense, and it was a simple one—an emotional withdrawal from the proceedings. Riley knew that he was the important one and talked directly to him.

"You took the food, Boris?" he asked in a voice that held no accusation. Boris gave no change of expression yet seemed to ponder the question. Allen added, "We found some of it in your bunk."

The slightest shrug went through the boy's shoulders. "Yes, I took some," he said.

"Why?" Allen asked. "You have plenty to eat. Why did you take the rations out of the lifeboats?"

"To give to my starving parents when I get home," the boy said.

With that single sentence he had blunted the attack. He was now the dutiful son worrying about his parents; he was acting from the highest of motives, not the lowest. No one could censure him for such filial concern.

Allen heard the calculation in the words, saw the mask of innocence on the boy's face, yet was powerless before them. To denounce them as false would not really destroy them, it would only put him in the position of being a man without logic and, worse, without heart.

"Boris," he said gently, "it will be a long time before you see your parents. And when you are finally able to, we shall prepare food packages for you to take to them. In the meantime, it is important for you, for all of us, that the food in the lifeboats be undisturbed. If there is ever an accident to this ship and we have to row away in those boats and there isn't any food, we'd be in real trouble, wouldn't we?"

The rest of the boys accepted the logic of Allen's words and nodded their heads in agreement. But not Boris. He looked back impassively, neither accepting nor rejecting. He had made his statement and he knew it was sufficient to the problem.

Finally Allen expressed the belief that such pilfering would not happen again and dismissed the boys. After they had filed out of his cabin, he turned to Walker who had been sitting in the background with Bramhall, and said, "Ward, I'm going to appoint you police officer for the voyage. I would suggest the advisability of setting up a night security watch on deck."

"Yes, sir," Walker said. "I'll stand the night watch myself."

"We could all take turns, but I think it would be well to involve some of the others who may not have as much to do. How about some of the Czechs?"

"I'll talk to them," Ward said.

The success of the girls' chorus was taken as a challenge by the boys' stringed orchestra and they announced they would give a concert on the following evening, July 17. Everybody gathered on deck at eight o'clock, full of eager anticipation, and when the members of the orchestra walked into the cleared circle there was great applause. The boys, about thirty of them, gave little bows and grinned happily at the acclaim. From that moment on, however, there was some confusion.

The truth was, the orchestra was not ready for its public debut. The Red Cross had obtained the balalaikas and mandolins and guitars only a few weeks before sailing and the musicians were not yet masters of their instruments. At this moment, though, they seemed completely unaware of that fact. They seated themselves in a semicircle, held their instruments confidently on their laps and looked at the eighteen-year-old concert master for a downbeat. He gave it with a sharp jerk of his head and the opening chord burst forth, held for a moment of shattering disharmony, then faded away.

The musicians looked at each other reproachfully, for they were obviously not playing the same number. There was a hurried consultation, finally agreement, and a fresh start. This time they got under way with some degree of unanimity and plunged ahead with verve. It was soon clear, however, that the tempo was too fast and some of the musicians could not maintain the pace. A few simply quit, others paused as if to catch their breath, then attempted to jump ahead and rejoin. In this kind of musical hopscotch it was most difficult to come in on the right note, and the discords produced tended to disorient even those who had maintained the race. Despite the furious stamping of the concert master's foot to keep the tempo, the music faltered and then faded to a few plaintive notes, then into silence.

There were some giggles from the girls in the audience, but before its contagion could spread, Mother Campbell jumped to her feet and spoke to them all in Russian. She congratulated the orchestra on attempting such a difficult piece and thanked them for allowing them all to listen to a rehearsal. She suggested that they play it again, slower this time, and finish it. The important thing was to play it to the end, no matter what the difficulties. She would be the conductor, she announced, and raised her arms to bring them to attention.

The boys were reluctant to undertake the piece a second time but there was no denying Mother Campbell, and when she gave the downbeat they responded. Her tempo turned out to be a bit ragged, but it was slow and it was determined. Together they made it through the piece, the musicians ending with a unanimous crescendo.

There was applause and laughter from the audience. The laughter was pleasure and pride. In its way, the concert had been a success and everyone went to bed feeling happy that there had been no surrender.

No, not everyone was happy. Allen entered in the log that night: ". . . This band proved so strong in volume and comparatively so weak on quality that the captain objected that his sailors could not sleep and we will have to move the band away from the sailors' quarters."

On July 21, the log read: "We are having considerable difficulty with the . . . boys aboard who are devoting their energy and inventive minds to stealing all sorts of things, including food supplies and clothing . . . as a number of them have been in the habit of stealing things since before the American Red Cross took hold of the colony, they are almost as skillful as adult criminals."

Shortly after making this entry Allen called Hal Davison into his office and said, "Hal, I can foresee that we're going to have a lot of trouble with some of the boys. It seems to me wise if we isolate the more obstreperous ones and have them live apart with one of our adult staff. It's not a pleasant or easy assignment but I'm asking you to undertake it."

A casual inspection of Hal Davison would seem to disqualify him for such stern duty. He was a physician, a small-boned man with a delicate and gentle face. He wore steel-rimmed spectacles over blue eyes that were often quizzical. He was aboard with his Russian bride, Natalia Alexeyevna Beklemisheva, who had been a member of the Czarist Russian Red Cross and had volunteered in Vladivostok to assist with the Colony. Davison had done remarkable work in primitive Siberian posts, but he was essentially a healer, not a disciplinarian.

And yet, Allen had been shrewd in his choice. Hal Davison was firm and direct. He talked little but to the point, and whenever he said "No," the word was both unequivocal and reasonable. In short, he would be respected by the boys, and he would be demanding of them.

A special part of No. 5 hold was set aside for the troublemakers and Hal Davison moved down into it and lived with them the rest of the trip. Whatever happened henceforth, the trouble would have been doubly explosive except for the presence of this physician.

SIXTEEN

Each day produced a mixed bag of good and bad, progression and regression. Nor could the staff hope to anticipate even half of what was to occur, for the events stemmed from the facts of life, the natural laws of growth through which the 780 children were going. Thus were the younger children innocent and at the same time savages. The eight- to eleven-year-olds could be good and cooperative and thoughtful, then quixotically selfish and destructive and deceitful. And the adolescents were gamblers with life, throwing themselves into strange attitudes just to see what would happen.

On Friday, July 23, at the second sitting of lunch, the older girls from hold No. 2 suddenly began to bang their cups on the tables and chant in unison, "The food is fit for pigs." Only a handful of them started the chant but soon it was taken up by all.

Maria Gorbochova was a monitor for this group and she stood up and clapped her hands over her head for attention. All the girls looked at her and grinned but kept up the chant.

"Stop! Stop!" Maria pleaded. "Please stop it."

But they did not stop. They were having too much fun,

getting too much attention. Maria looked around for help and saw Mother Campbell step out of the galley. She rushed up to her with an apology on her lips, but Mother Campbell was grinning and brushed her words aside. At this moment Ward Walker came striding up.

"There's a disturbance going on here," he announced with a frown.

"So I hear," Mother Campbell replied.

"Well, I'm going to stop it."

She held out a restraining hand. "I notice that their plates are empty. They demonstrate *after* eating so they can't think the food is too bad."

"We can't have this sort of thing aboard a crowded ship."

"It won't last long," she assured him. "They're just letting off a little steam. And you know about boilers, Ward. Never tie down the safety valve."

"I know about insolence, too," he said darkly.

"Oh, pooh!" Mother Campbell replied.

By now the girls had attracted quite an audience of staff and crew members and they made the most of it. They began to bang their cups on the tables in the rhythm of their chant. At last Mother Campbell came forward and took a position in the center of the dining area, put her hands on her hips and slowly turned about to look at them with an impassive face. The girls stared back with some anxiety. Suddenly Mother Campbell began to laugh. She threw back her head and gave out a whoop of laughter. It startled the girls into sudden silence. This was the last thing they had expected and they didn't know what to make of it. They responded unthinkingly—they began to laugh too. Soon the entire area echoed to the shouts of delight. When at last they calmed a bit, Mother Campbell spoke to them.

"The food is fit for pigs, you say? Well, we all know there's a few pigs on this ship and maybe we ought to try it out on them."

Everyone laughed again. For some reason the remark

seemed excruciatingly funny and each girl thought of her own candidate for pig.

"Seriously," Mother Campbell said, "I *have* eaten better tasting food in my day. But that was when I was home and could take time to do things properly. We have a problem here aboard ship. The galley is not arranged in the most efficient manner, we don't have enough help, and we have a lot of mouths to feed. Now, I have a suggestion. Why don't you girls give me a hand in the galley? You could divide into platoons, some helping with breakfast, some with lunch and some with supper. What do you say to that? How many are with me?"

Every hand shot into the air. During the rest of the trip the girls helped efficiently and cheerfully in the galley. And there was not another demonstration against the food.

At the inception of this trip there had been some apprehension expressed about the possible misconduct of the prisoners of war. All such fears turned out to be groundless, for the P.O.W.'s were continuously busy and cheerful. They worked during the day mainly as kitchen and messroom help under the direction of Mother Campbell, and for this Clarence Rowland paid them a small weekly wage. To augment this income they did handicraft work on deck at night in their own time. Many of them had brought pieces of copper aboard which they shaped skillfully into small matchboxes or larger cigar boxes, with a button off their uniforms soldered to the top. They sold these souvenirs to the American personnel and Japanese crew members at a lively rate, building for themselves small nest eggs.

When they finally did get home, inflation was raging in all the countries of the Central Powers and a suit of clothes could be purchased for five American dollars. The P.O.W.'s from the *Yomei Maru* wound up being among the best dressed people in Middle Europe.

Friday, July 30, the log read: ". . . Found it necessary today to decree Monday, and Monday only, as washday. Several hundred people, mostly the Colony girls and women person-

nel, have a mania for washing their clothes and hanging them
on any adjacent peg or rope, with the result that parts of our
good ship *Yomei Maru* were assuming the aspect of Hogan's
Alley on a sunny morning in May. We have now set apart the
poop deck and every Monday for the devotees of the tub and
washboard. While their zeal and cleanliness is certainly com-
mendable, it must be restricted to one part of the ship."

The weather remained mild and the *Yomei Maru* continued
to slip through calm waters, flying her wash, trailing a babble
of childish voices. However, there were storm clouds gathering, though they were not the sort that registered on the ship's
barometer. There set in a deterioration of the relationship between the children and the ship's crew. There were only small
things at first, petty annoyances, but each one added some
specific weight to what was first alienation, and then hostility.

Riley Allen watched this development with some anxiety
and while he was quick to move in upon each smoldering
incident, he was unable to smother the underlying causes.

Boswell once wrote, "Being in a ship is like being in jail,
with the chance of being drowned."

Though the weather was good, the crew could not help
speculating upon the possible consequences of a storm, the
abandonment of the ship, the chaos that would overwhelm
them if 780 children became panic-stricken. They didn't like
this cargo, this voyage. Moreover, they were separated from
the children by the barrier of language, by the barrier of age,
and most of all by the barrier of history. The Russo-Japanese
War was but fifteen years gone. At this very moment Japanese
soldiers were attempting to wrest the Maritime Provinces from
Russia. It seemed ironic to the crew that they should be engaged in taking Russian children home to Petrograd where
they might one day grow up and fight the Japanese.

All the dark currents of history reached out to swirl about
the *Yomei Maru* in the middle of the sun-dappled Pacific.
Riley Allen walked lightly, slept little, and counted on the

discipline and good sense of Captain Kayahara. At least he did until the events of Saturday, July 31.

Saturday nights are special to children the world over. It is a night to stay up late, to have a party, to enjoy some of the adult privileges. All details of the Saturday night dance aboard the *Yomei Maru* had been discussed and agreed upon between Allen and Captain Kayahara and there was no reason to believe any problems would turn up.

There was great anticipation among the children during the day, and excited pairing off among the older boys and girls. The orchestra, which had made such an inauspicious debut, had practiced almost daily and looked forward to vindication on this night. The prisoners of war and the Russian and American staffs welcomed this break in routine. During the regular morning conference with Captain Kayahara, Riley Allen had requested that special lights be strung on the deck so that the musicians might better read their music. This was done.

The dance began at eight o'clock. First there was a set piece by the orchestra, and they all finished at the same time on the same note. A good omen for the evening, and it brought great applause from the crowded deck. Now came time for a hopak to be danced by the children in groups. The younger ones formed first in a circle, and as the music struck up, they moved clockwise, stomping to the rhythm, bending and straightening, first on their heels and then on their toes, their faces shining with happy excitement. As the older groups took their turns the tempo increased and the shouts grew louder and soon all the spectators were clapping to the rhythm.

The music became infectious and dancing broke out all over the deck, sometimes with amazing results. Some Czechs began to dance a polka, the Hungarians attempted a galop, here and there the Americans entered into a fox trot, all to the Russian rhythms. It made no difference if the steps failed to match the music's tempo, the two matched in spirit—the physical expression of the joy of being alive.

Suddenly there was an angry shout. Amid the noise of the

music and the stamping feet and the laughter it was all but lost, and for a moment no one was quite sure it had been made. But then it came again, louder and choking with rage. The musicians glanced up, lost their places in the music, faltered and then quit. The stamping became a shuffle and then stilled. The ship's first officer, wearing his kimono, stood in the open door of his cabin. His legs were spread, his arms akimbo, his face contorted. He glared at the dancers until he had their complete attention, then he let loose a violent denunciation. The words were in Japanese, but the tone was unmistakable.

Riley Allen moved quickly out of the crowd and walked up to the officer. "What is the trouble?" he asked.

The man repeated his tirade—in Japanese.

"You can speak English, sir," Riley Allen said. "Please do so."

In English the officer announced that he could not sleep and he demanded an immediate end to the dance. Allen looked at his watch. It was nine forty-five. He said, "By agreement between Captain Kayahara and myself the Saturday dances are to continue until ten-thirty."

Each word inflamed the Japanese officer to an even greater heat. His rage seemed entirely out of proportion to the problem. Allen said, "I'm sorry your sleep has been disturbed, but the dance will be over in forty-five minutes."

For a long moment the officer balanced himself on the balls of his feet and seemed to consider a number of actions. Finally, with a thunderous look, he whirled and went back into his cabin, slamming the metal door behind him with such violence as to send a hollow boom over the hushed decks.

Allen turned to the musicians and nodded that they could continue the music. The dancing resumed, though not with such a carefree air. Allen walked back to his place and leaned against the starboard rail. About five minutes went by and then a figure moved out of the shadows and stood beside him. It was Captain Kayahara.

"Good evening, Captain," Allen said.

The captain gave a slight, formal bow. "I should like to know," he said, "how late you intend the dance to continue."

"Why, until ten-thirty, Captain. Just as you and I agreed."

"Thank you," the captain said. Then he disappeared back into the shadows.

Several other matters occupied Allen for the next minutes. Mother Campbell conferred with him about the next day's menu, the quartermaster wanted to discuss an inventory of supplies, and the treasurer, Clarence Rowland, reported the completion of the weekly payments to children and staff and P.O.W. employees.

Perhaps eight minutes were thus consumed when Dr. Eversole strode up to him with a look of concern on his face. "I was just up on the poop deck," he said, "and the captain is pacing back and forth, furious about the dance."

"Did he speak to you about it?"

"I should say he did! He threatened that as soon as we hit the States he might cancel the voyage and return the *Yomei Maru* to Japan."

Allen pursed his lips and looked at the whirling dancers and the furiously playing mandolins. Bramhall joined them now and Eversole repeated the information.

"Riley," Bramhall said, "can he do that? I mean, we do have a charter on this ship. Can the captain abrogate it?"

"I don't know," Allen said.

As they pondered the question the captain suddenly appeared, elbowing his way brusquely through the dancers. He threw a dark look toward the three Red Cross officials and disappeared on forward. In a few moments he reappeared and again scattered dancers unceremoniously as he made his way aft.

"Maybe you'd better go speak to him, Riley," Bramhall said.

"I think not," Allen said. "Not when he's in this mood. What we don't want right now is a showdown over a trivial issue."

"Good lord, look at that!" Eversole suddenly exclaimed. "I thought he was kidding."

Through the dancers now came Japanese sailors carrying an empty kerosene barrel. They went aft to the poop deck with it.

Eversole said, "Riley, he threatened to get a metal barrel and beat it outside your cabin tonight after you went to bed. You don't suppose he'd do such a childish thing?"

"I don't know but we can't take a chance. I'm going to cancel the dance."

"Riley . . ." Bramhall objected.

"We can't let the captain make a fool of himself," Allen said. "Such actions would only encourage the worst elements of the crew, would weaken his authority over them. That could be disastrous. No, I'll have to cancel."

Allen strode to the middle of the dance area, raised his arms for attention and announced it was the end of the dance and everyone should return to quarters. Some of the older children shouted that it was only ten-fifteen but Allen was firm. The teachers sensed an urgency in him and soon had their charges moving toward the hatches.

The musicians packed up their instruments, folded their chairs, stacked them and lashed them down. A cleanup detail swept up the paper cups that had held the fruit juice punch. The specially rigged lights were extinguished. At ten forty-five the decks were clear and quiet. Allen made a last tour of inspection and then went into his cabin. The *Yomei Maru* looked as she had on every other night of this voyage, except for one thing—the grotesquerie of an empty kerosene barrel that sat outside the captain's door.

Once in his cabin, Allen began to enter in the log a full report of the evening's events. He filled several pages, then concluded with: "I saw the Captain around the decks but purposely did not take up the issue, which might easily have been made serious. Because of his remarks to Dr. Eversole I purposely let him alone . . . to allow him to cool down, having felt from several previous instances that he is apt to grow quite angry and then to get over it . . . I am devoting so

much space in the log to this incident as I do not believe it will
be the last . . ."

Through the long dark hours the barrel remained mute but
threatening. With the dawn there arrived something that banished all thoughts of the barrel—San Francisco arrived!

To sail into safe harbor after a long time at sea is an exhila-
rating experience. However calm the passage may have been,
the voyager is constantly aware of the awesome power of the
ocean, its potential violence, and to have challenged it and
survived makes a man feel godlike. With firm land suddenly
beneath his feet, with the horizon leveled, with the world ordered, there comes a euphoria that wipes away the recent fears
and hates.

Thus it is that any port is beautiful, but San Francisco is a
very special one. As the *Yomei Maru* slid through the welcoming arms of the Golden Gate and into the inner harbor, the
children were dazzled by the whiteness of the hillside city.
Their own towns were drab and dirty, and this seemed like
something out of a fairy story. "They must scrub it every day,"
they said excitedly to each other.

The local chapters of the Red Cross had prepared an elaborate civic welcome and the waterfront was jammed with people
as the ship nudged her dock. In the excitement, fourteen-year-
old Vera Milhailova fell overboard and into the harbor. A San
Francisco policeman immediately dived in and rescued her, to
the cheers of the crowd. It seemed to the city, and to the
children, that this was a highly symbolic act and it set the tone
of goodwill and brotherhood for the subsequent days.

As the children disembarked to be taken by bus to Fort
Winfield Scott where they were to stay in the army barracks,
they were met by representatives of the Junior Red Cross and
given fruit, candy and toys. The next afternoon there was a
public ceremony in front of City Hall where they were welcomed by the mayor and other civic leaders. That evening they
were entertained by a musical program in the Civic Audi-

torium. As a gesture of thanks, the Colony's chorus and orchestra and dancers also performed.

On the following day the entire Colony was transported to Golden Gate Park where all the amusement concessions were opened to them free of charge. They swung and looped and circled and jiggled and ate hot dogs. All the time they were surrounded by admiring throngs who forced presents into their hands.

During these days in San Francisco the children saw some of America's finest qualities—openheartedness, generosity, and a wish for justice to waifs of war and revolution. There was nothing contrived or self-seeking in the outpourings of affection and gifts. For the moment their days were sunny.

The afternoon of August 4 the Colony reboarded the *Yomei Maru* and on the following morning, with a band playing and thousands lining the shore to wave farewell, the ship backed off from her dock, came about and headed out through the Golden Gate and then south toward the Panama Canal. Captain Kayahara had not carried out his threat to return the ship to Japan.

The passions that had generated aboard ship during the Pacific crossing had been largely drained off during the freedom on land, but now back in the confinement of the sea they began to build again. That this overloaded ship was headed into the sweltering tropics was a fact far from reassuring. And most unsettling of all was that Riley Allen was not aboard. Much as his coolness was needed aboard the *Yomei Maru*, it was needed even more in Washington where the Red Cross had been plunged into a profound policy crisis.

SEVENTEEN

It was August when Riley Allen arrived in Washington, D.C., and a damp, tropical haze pressed upon the city, wilting collars and burning feet and shortening tempers. This happened every August, but in this year of 1920 there were added reasons why the nation's capital was a cauldron of rumor, sweat and frustration.

America was exhausted from the greatest war in its history. It was tired of idealism, tired of sacrifice, and dismayed over the fact that the recent outpouring of both had not ordered the world but left it more turbulent than before. The people wished for a return to the quiet days, the uncomplicated days that had existed prior to World War I. Warren Harding was campaigning successfully on a platform of "back to normalcy."

The people found it difficult to say exactly what "normalcy" was, for it sprang from nostalgia, from evanescent dreams, but they were pretty clear on what it was *not*. It was not idealists who wanted to reorganize other people's lives; it was not foreign entanglements, not the League of Nations; it was not Bolshevik agitators who kept stirring things up instead of letting them settle back to the "good old days."

Sacco and Vanzetti were in prison this August, not so much because the public believed them guilty of the Braintree bombing, but because they were most certainly guilty of being radical agitators guilty of a conspiracy to prevent America's returning to "normalcy."

It was in this prevailing national mood of disillusionment that the American Red Cross had to decide what to do with 780 children from Petrograd, city of Bolshevik revolution. Riley Allen had been operating under the simple formula of returning the children to their parents, wherever they might be and whatever their politics. But when he got to Washington he found that the problem was much more complex and subtle than it had appeared at Vladivostok.

The arrival of the children in San Francisco had been well publicized and their fate was the subject of great editorial speculation. It became a matter of concern to the War Department and to the State Department, and conflicting counsel came from both of them. The Red Cross was free to makes its own decisions, but it could not ignore the possible consequences of any decision. And where it had the right to expect strong leadership, from its own president, there was silence. For the president of the Red Cross was also the President of the United States, and Woodrow Wilson lay mortally ill.

The men upon whom rested the major responsibility for decision were Dr. Livingston Farrand, chairman of the Red Cross Central Committee, and Frederick P. Keppel, vice-chairman and director of the Bureau of Foreign Operations. It was to them that Allen argued his case that they had a moral commitment to return the children to their parents and any conscious delay by so much as a day would plunge the Red Cross deeper into the political morass from which they all longed to escape.

In opposition to Allen's position was Robert E. Olds, Red Cross European Commissioner, and he made a formidable case for delay. Writing to Farrand from his office in Paris, Olds expressed himself:

. . . We cannot bring ourselves to the conclusion that under existing circumstances any attempt should be made to repatriate the children in wholesale fashion. There are various objections to such a course. One is that many of the parents and relatives who have an obvious right to be consulted are no longer in Soviet Russia. They have been driven out and are refugees in various neutral and allied countries. These persons would bitterly resent the sending of their children into Soviet Russia. Already one man has called at our office and discovered his child on the list. In this connection it should be remembered that some of the boys have already reached the age of sixteen or seventeen and are liable to be placed at once in military service if they are sent back. All things considered, therefore, I cannot see that it would be just to repatriate the children in a body in response to a sweeping demand from the Soviet authorities; and we feel that such a course would bring upon the American Red Cross an avalanche of criticism possibly rising to the dignity of a scandal. We are bound to get some criticism out of the whole thing. We would do better to face a continuance of the Bolshevik propaganda against us than to face the still more violent, and much better founded, criticism which would certainly be leveled at us by the parents and relatives of a certain number of the children if we should indulge in a wholesale, immediate repatriation.

Our view in this regard, followed to a logical conclusion, would mean that the children should be held under our immediate control somewhere for a sufficiently long period of time to permit discriminatory action. If it can be established that a large number of the children have parents now in Soviet Russia who really want to have their children sent to them, I can see no reason why requests from such parents should be denied. Colonel Ryan, however, is very suspicious of the so-called "Parents Association" in Petrograd. He thinks it is very likely a camouflaged association, put up by the Government. It is also possible that the Government does not itself really wish to have the children sent back but is capitalizing on the existing situation for propaganda purposes. . . .

. . . Assuming that we are to hold the children . . . the question of the location of the children in Europe for a sufficient period of time becomes vastly important. In that event, we must contemplate holding some of the children, perhaps a considerable number, for many months, perhaps throughout the coming winter although we should hope to wind up the whole business this Fall and should bend every energy to that end. Colonel Ryan, who has just been to Paris, advises me that he can take these children and care for them almost indefinitely in the Baltic Provinces provided his Unit is kept up on substantially its present basis and his resources are not altogether dissipated by shipments to other Commissions. He points out nevertheless that there are some serious objections to carrying on the enterprise just now in Latvia or in any other of the States or countries negotiating with the Soviet Government. For example, the negotiations between Latvia and Esthonia on the one hand and the Bolsheviks on the other, are still going on. The states so negotiating would clearly be embarrassed by a demand for the immediate surrender of these children if they were located within their borders. It is possible that the Soviet Government might insist upon some stipulation in pending treaties covering this subject. It might offer a readjustment of boundary in order to get the surrender of the children. This objection is not conclusive but is entitled to urgent consideration. The argument in favor of putting the children within the territorial limits of a country which could not possibly be embarrassed by any formal demand from Moscow is pretty strong. As we look at the thing now we should be inclined to set these children down in France. We know that we could care for them here; we know that our control over the whole situation would be far more effective under such circumstances; and we know that the inquiries which we have in mind would, for obvious reasons, be conducted more expeditiously from France than from any other place in Europe.

Commissioner Olds was in error when he stated that many of the parents had left Petrograd. When the facts were ultimately established it was discovered that only a small percentage of them had done so. The commissioner was guilty of some wishful thinking. In a subsequent letter to Dr. Farrand he stated his case against repatriation of the children in even stronger terms:

The Russians here in France are tremendously interested and they are bringing us daily reports indicating that the conditions in Russia doom most of the children to almost certain death if they are sent in now. Some of these men who have talked to us have children in Russia whom they cannot get out and whom they have not heard from for many months —in some cases years. There are Russians here who have recently succeeded in getting out of the country and they speak of the conditions as absolutely intolerable at the present time. They insist that continued American Red Cross control is essential if the children are to survive and get fair treatment.

. . . It is difficult, by letter, to put the case before you properly. We, of course, apply a liberal discount to all reports that come to us, but after making due allowance for the emotional factor, the bare facts are impressive enough. We are confident that no children sent in to Moscow or Petrograd today can expect to find decent living conditions. We believe, from all of the evidence in our possession now, that the prospect that any appreciable number of such children would be brought in contact with their parents is remote and problematical . . . There is no freedom of movement in Russia in these times and about the best that could happen to a colony of children landing in Petrograd would be to become an orphanage under Government patronage . . . It is more than likely that the children would have to face all degrees of hardship and degradation down to the point of disease, famine and death. We are told by our Russian friends here that every boy able to carry a gun will find himself conscripted for the Red Army without a moment's delay. As for girls fifteen years and over, they simply shrug their shoulders. The little children, they assert, cannot conceivably get food and care which they must have in order to survive.

The question inevitably arises whether an institution of the standards and ideals of the American Red Cross can discharge its responsibilities by sending a group of eight hundred children, to whom it has stood in the relation of guardian for a considerable period, to face such conditions. It is not at all a political issue. The considerations are of a purely humanitarian character. If the testimony were conflicting we might justify the course suggested, but every scrap of reliable evidence we can get militates against this action. . . .

. . . It does not require much imagination to see that whatever we do we shall become the object of violent attack and bitter recrimnation. If any arrangement is made to hold the children, either in France or elsewhere, we must expect to be the target for Soviet propaganda, and if we send the children to Petrograd and Moscow we shall be charged with "throwing them to the wolves." One does not like to think of the feelings of parents, now in France, Finland or Switzerland, who discover a few weeks hence that their children have been sent by the American Red Cross into the country from which they have fled for their lives. . . .

Robert Olds was a respected and high official of the Red Cross and his strongly stated opinions could not help having great weight with the Central Committee as it made its agonized appraisal.

EIGHTEEN

The *Yomei Maru* was headed south along the Pacific coast and into tropic waters. The overwhelming fact of life aboard her was the heat. Unlike the Washington heat which was damp, here on the sea it was dry and harsh and pounded down upon the ship like a brassy fist.

The heat complicated every activity, frayed every human relationship. Disciplinary problems with the children became more frequent and more difficult of solution. Day by day the crew grew more sullen.

In Riley Allen's absence, seniority had given Dr. Eversole command of the Colony and with Bramhall at his side he attempted to seal over each small eruption as it occurred. It was Eversole who kept the log.

By August 9, four days out of San Francisco, the log began to reveal the tensions generated by the heat: "Because we have two children who are demented and there is no place on the ship which is quiet for them, we have asked the children to give up the port side of the poop deck for these invalids . . . The weather has become progressively hotter until at four o'clock in the afternoon it was 130 in the kitchens and 105 under the canvas on the decks with a temperature of 88 in the hatches . . . Many of the children decided to sleep on deck and even brought their beds out and began to settle themselves, but on account of the small number for which there is room on deck, and because it made such a disturbance . . . we found it necessary to send them all to their bunks . . . The photographer, Mr. Faitzer, has made numerous negatives of the children during the past few days, and asked me to request the captain to turn on the electricity in the darkroom. I asked the captain and he said it was on every night. I told him I was sorry to inform him he was mistaken, that it had not been on since leaving San Francisco. He gave instructions to one of his officers that it should be turned on this evening. As I went down the stairs, I happened to look back and the captain was making grotesque signs and laughing with the officer to whom he had just given the order . . . the electricity was not turned on in the darkroom during the evening . . . Between 6:00 and 10:00 P.M. there were ten boys admitted to the hospital with a temperature of 103, and nauseated from 'heat stroke.' They were packed in ice . . ."

Games and dances and calisthenics, previously a major part of play and diversion, were now prohibited and inactivity made the days interminable.

Some of the older boys became insolent to the Russian staff and this was reported to Eversole by the head teacher, De-George. Eversole called the boys before him to express his disappointment.

"These teachers have done so much for you," he said, "have been so loyal. They have shared all your hardships . . ."

"Not any more," one of the boys interrupted. "We are forced to sleep in the hold while they sleep on the cool deck. They don't share our lives any more and so they don't deserve our respect."

Resentment festered in almost everyone aboard the *Yomei Maru*. Bramhall and Eversole could only hope for a break in the weather. But none was to come, at least not in time. Before they were through the Panama Canal two crises exploded aboard the sweltering ship. Both involved the children and the crew.

There were many adolescent girls aboard the *Yomei Maru* but the most blooming was, perhaps, Natasha Lebedeva. She was a willowy child of fifteen who seemed to embrace womanhood suddenly with none of the dark fears and introspection that often accompany the process. Hers was an open, happy welcoming. She walked proudly, her shoulders thrown back and her young breasts thrust forward against the confining fabric of her blouse. She was aware of the glances of the older boys but she was neither offended nor titillated; she accepted them as a tribute. She was utterly without coquetry.

She was glad to be a woman because it was the necessary first step to being a mother. She wanted two girls and three boys. If she thought of the mechanics of becoming a mother, she concluded they must be romantic and beautiful. Nothing with so glorious an end result as children could be anything but beautiful.

There was a crew member who watched Natasha from a distance. He was a stoker, shoveled coal in the engine room, and during his time off he lounged about on deck and followed her with his eyes. If she had noticed him she would have seen nothing but an impassive face; she had not the experience to read what was in his eyes.

Natasha's bunk was in No. 2 hold and it was necessary for the engine room crew to pass through the hold on the way down to work, and again on the way back up after work. The stoker who had been watching her so avidly was on the middle watch, midnight to 4 A.M. He developed a habit of arriving a few minutes late, coming down alone. The man he was to relieve complained to the chief engineer about it and he was reprimanded.

At 12:05 A.M. on the morning of August 10, a scream rang through the dark, heated air of No. 2 hold. In the moment of silence that followed, there was a slither of quick steps and

then the babble of awakening girls. A teacher appeared and
turned on the lights. All eyes went to Natasha Lebedeva who
sat erect in her bunk, her face white and set. It was she who
had screamed but she couldn't now explain why. She had been
asleep and it must have been some nightmare. After a time the
rest of the girls calmed down and the lights were put out.

Natasha lay wide-eyed in her bunk and wondered what had
happened to make her wake up screaming. She felt as if she
had been handled. She couldn't explain to herself why this
feeling, but it was there, all over her. It was a horrible feeling,
like nothing she had ever before known. She felt sickish.

The teacher who had come down to investigate, Seraphina
Victorova, guessed what had happened, for she had been
wakeful and walking the deck and had seen the stoker go into
No. 2 hold. When Natasha insisted that she had screamed in a
nightmare, the teacher did not press her but the next morning
she reported the occurrence to Dr. Eversole.

In the log under the date of August 10, Dr. Eversole eu-
phemistically reported that the seaman had touched Natasha's
"shoulder." Then he wrote:

"I immediately took this up with the captain and he promised to stop his men walking through the hatch. . . ."

Throughout that day Natasha was quiet and withdrawn.
The mood of the nightmare seemed to enfold her. When it was
bedtime she went below with the others and lay down on her
bunk but she refused to shut her eyes, for she was determined
to remain awake through the night and thus prevent the return
of the nightmare. But despite herself she dozed off around
eleven-thirty.

Shortly after midnight Natasha was half-awake and half-
asleep when she felt a scream building within her. But she
hesitated a moment, for she wanted desperately to know what
was real and what was dream. And with the scream bottled up
in her throat she felt the hands go over her. They were smooth
and quick and possessed of a terrible accuracy. She struck out
and hit the solid flesh of an arm. It was no dream, but reality.

The scream ripped out of her throat and the hands disappeared. Yet they seemed still upon her and she screamed again and again.

The following day the log contained Eversole's report: ". . . One of the educators came to me quite excited and complained that the Japanese sailors had continued to walk through the aisles between the bunks occupied by our larger girls and had turned the flashlight directly on the girls during their passage and that one of them had again put his arms around the same girl whom he had molested the night before . . . she was quite ill this morning from the fright he had given her. I immediately went to the captain and in very plain words told him that he must immediately call his men who were on night duty and talk to them in such a manner that they would understand that if he could not control them, we would have to take it upon ourselves to put them under surveillance."

Passengers threatening to put a crew under surveillance was a move fraught with infinite dangers. But the failure to make such a threat could lead to equal or even greater dangers, and Dr. Eversole was acting under the dictates of his principal responsibility—the welfare of the children.

During the confrontation Captain Kayahara stood with his hands clasped rigidly behind him, his face stony. He was being told that he did not have control of his own men, and it was a bitter thing for him to hear. He made no protest, however, for the only alternative conclusion would be that he abetted their actions. He announced that such actions would stop. And stop they did. But it was clear to everyone, including the crew, that Captain Kayahara had lost considerable face. And this too was a dangerous thing to have happen.

As for the illness that had struck Natasha, it never left her. It was the illness of spirit. She now walked with rounded shoulders, without pride in her new womanhood. The Red Cross staff gave her tender and loving attention but they could not take from her the searing knowledge that life contained some ugly things.

The heat continued without letup, pulling the sweat and the salt and some of the sense out of the *Yomei Maru's* human cargo. The log noted: "It is necessary to stop the motors two or three times a day . . . on account of the intense heat in the motor room . . . we find it necessary to stop all the motors from 2:00 P.M. to 3:30 P.M. for overhauling and cooling. We chose . . . [that] hour because there is no reason why all of the children cannot be on deck at that time, and it gives the balance of the afternoon and evening to cool the hatches again."

On August 12 the log noted: "It was necessary to detail a strong guard of two boys on the poop deck to assist the nurses with the boy who is demented, Vladimir Maligin. The nurses felt they might not be strong enough to handle him in case he carried out his threat to jump overboard."

With almost the entire ship's company on deck seeking relief from the heat, the children tended to spill over into areas that the crew considered their own. Ilin Kartasheff was one such boy who spilled over.

Ilin was a hulking sixteen-year-old with a head of tight blond curls above a square, good-natured face. He was heavy of foot, with an awkward, loping gait, and tended to knock over the salt and pepper at mealtime whenever he reached for something with his thick, freckled hands. He was a bright enough boy but his heavy structure seemed to prevent any but the grossest coordination.

One afternoon he wandered up to the boat deck, normally reserved for the crew. Outside the galley a Japanese cook squatted on his heels and pared potatoes into a large metal pot. Against the deckhouse there was a rope locker that consumed part of the space, but even so there was a good yard of passageway. Most anybody could have negotiated it, but not Ilin Kartasheff. His big foot caught on the handle of the pot, tipping it on edge and sending two dozen white, slick potatoes skidding across the deck and into the scuppers. With a guttural cry of rage, the cook leaped upon Ilin's back and began to pummel him. The boy shook him off, whirled around and the two faced each other in a crouch, fists raised for combat.

Henry Wood, the recreation officer, happened by at this moment and stepped between them. "Ilin, nyet!" he commanded.

The boy dropped his fists and stood erect. While the cook stood aside, Wood and Ilin righted the pot and returned all the potatoes to it. Then they went to find Eversole and report the occurrence.

The doctor listened to the report, then said, "You acted with good judgment, Wood. The simplest friction with the crew can lead to grave consequences. Did you have Ilin apologize to the cook?"

"Yes, sir, but I don't think the cook understood anything we were saying. It was all an accident, and not anything Ilin meant to do."

"Of course. But I think the boy and I had better call upon Captain Kayahara and explain things firsthand. You come along, just in case he questions my account of the events."

And so there was another of the frequent and painful meetings with the captain. Kayahara listened rather distantly, as if advantage were being taken of his time and his patience.

Eversole completed his report and said, "The boy would like to apologize directly to the cook if you would supply us with a translator."

"There is no need," the captain said airily. "I will take care of the matter."

And on this equivocal note the meeting ended.

"We've done all we can for the moment," Eversole said to Wood as they left. "Let's hope this is the end of it."

But it wasn't—quite.

That evening Mother Campbell was walking the boat deck when she came upon the captain who was striding along with a belligerent look on his face and his hands thrust deep in his pockets. He seemed to be searching for something and Mother Campbell thought she'd be helpful.

"What are you looking for, Captain?"

"I've received a report that some of your boys are going to come up here where they don't belong. They may be hiding here now."

"Well, what are you going to do if you find them?"

"I'm going to shoot them," he said. "They can't act this way on my ship."

Mother Campbell took a quick look at his face, decided this was no time to try to reason with him, and scurried off in search of Bramhall and Eversole. She found them and the three of them returned to the boat deck, but there was no sign of the captain.

"You're certain he said he was going to *shoot* the boys?" Bramhall demanded.

"I sure am certain that's what he said," Mother Campbell declared.

"What language did he speak?" Eversole asked.

"Russian."

"Is his Russian good?"

"As good as mine," she said. "We understand each other."

Eversole turned to Bramhall. "What do you make of it?"

"Well, I don't think anything will be gained by a confrontation with him right now."

"Nor do I," Eversole agreed.

"We can assume that he expected Mother Campbell to report his words to us. That is his way of negotiating, by indirect threats."

"Damned unpleasant way."

"I'll get hold of Walker and see that he doubles the guard," Bramhall said. "I'll take a watch myself tonight, and stay at the foot of the companionway to the boat deck to make certain no boys get up there. I think that all the captain wants is a little privacy. And I don't suppose we can blame him for that."

"Humph!" Mother Campbell said.

Rain came on the following day. It was a tropical storm, slashing and short-lived, but it washed the decks and cooled the holds and seemed to soothe the raw nerve endings aboard the *Yomei Maru*. At the Red Cross staff meeting Mother Campbell said, "Let's have a dance tonight. It will be cool enough and I think the children need the diversion."

It was Saturday, August 21. The dance was to be held at 8 P.M. The trouble began at seven-thirty. And again Ilin Kartasheff was involved.

Ilin had approached the evening with eagerness and good-will. He was something of a menace on the dance floor because of his unfortunate combination of enthusiasm and awkwardness, but everyone made allowances for him. Everyone but the Japanese crew. They had heard the story of the potato pot; they apparently had not heard of his sincerely offered apology.

That evening as the musicians were setting up their music stands, Ilin and two friends strolled aft on the starboard side and came upon a small group of sailors. One of them stepped forward and in pantomime challenged Ilin to a wrestling match. He was smiling and seemed good-natured but Ilin was reluctant to accept. His companions urged him on, however, claiming that the honor of the Petrograd Colony was at stake. Put in that light, Ilin could not very well refuse, and the match began.

They circled, came together, gripped and strained, lost footing and regained it, broke apart and circled again. A crowd began to gather and it formed a large circle in which the contestants grappled. In each other's arms they fell to the deck and rolled about, each seeking to pin the other. It became clear that the sailor possessed more quickness and skill but Ilin had the advantage of weight. As a result they were fairly evenly matched.

After five minutes they lay gasping and locked together for a moment of rest. A change was taking place. In this alien body he clasped against his own, Ilin felt tremblings of mounting rage. Both the rage and the fear sent adrenaline into their bloodstreams and gave each more than his normal strength. When after a moment's rest, they resumed the contest it was with a terrible urgency. Hoarse sounds came from their throats as they strained together.

Ivan Kotovsky, one of the teachers, heard the sounds of the struggle and came to investigate. He pushed his way through the circle of spectators and saw the fierceness of the wrestling and decided it should be stopped. He called out to Ilin to stop and get up, but it was not easy for the boy to disentangle himself from his opponent unless they both ceased at the same time.

"Davolna . . . davolna!" Ilin gasped in the sailor's ear. "Enough . . . enough!"

The sailor did not, or would not, understand.

Even the boys became alarmed and they called, "Ilin, get up! It's time to go to the dance."

Ilin tore himself free and stood up, disheveled and panting. The sailor jumped to his feet and with a cry of rage, jumped at the boy, beating him with his fists. The two of them fell back to the deck in a wild scramble of arms and legs. It appeared to Kotovsky that the sailor had Ilin by the throat and was trying to strangle him. He grabbed the sailor by the shoulders, pulled him away from the boy. This action seemed to drive the sailor into an incoherent frenzy and he shouted and screamed and struck out at everyone.

Several of the crew tried to hold him but he broke loose to grab up a board from a coal bin and throw it at the teacher. The board fell short of its mark and clattered harmlessly on the deck. The crowd intervened and the sailor turned around and went aft.

"Everyone to the dance," Kotovsky shouted to the milling boys. "Time for the dance. Everyone forward."

The crowd was just beginning to break up when it was transfixed by a scream of rage. Everyone turned to find an apparition bearing down upon them. It was the returning sailor and his face was contorted and above his head he brandished a long knife. In another moment blood would surely flow, yet no one seemed capable of moving. Ilin, Kotovsky and the rest of the boys could only stare in horror.

As he was about to throw himself upon them, the sailor's own shipmates engulfed and bore him aft to their quarters. The boys, now released from the terror, scattered.

When this latest development was reported to Eversole, he held a worried conference with Bramhall. "There has to be a showdown with the captain," Bramhall said.

"I'm afraid so," Eversole agreed.

"At once! Tonight!" Bramhall urged. "This ship is a floating powder keg and the slightest spark can explode us. No one can control this crew but the captain and we've got to stiffen him, force him to do his job."

"I'll send word that we wish a meeting."

"I propose that we walk into his cabin unannounced and sit down. It will be a violation of protocol, but under the circumstances I think we must use a little calculated rudeness. We've got to impress upon him the seriousness of the situation."

Some minutes later Captain Kayahara looked up from his desk to see two grim-faced Americans. He was told what had happened and requested to hold an immediate inquiry. He agreed and since a fairly large number of people were to be involved, it was decided to hold the inquiry in the dining saloon.

Fifteen minutes later, with balalaika music drifting in the open portholes, the meeting was called to order. Present were Eversole, Bramhall, Walker, Kotovsky, Ilin and two other boys, and Miss Domerschikoff, a Russian teacher who would serve as interpreter. Also present were Captain Kayahara, the sailor who had drawn the sword, and three other sailors who had been present during the event.

Eversole demanded that the testimony of Ilin, Kotovsky and the boys be given first and a permanent record made of their words. This was done and all four stories were in substantial agreement as to the sequence of events.

"Now, sir," Eversole said to the captain, "I think your sailor should tell his side of the story."

The captain turned to his sailor who then put on a most astonishing performance. He shouted and pounded the table and seemed to lose all control of himself. The captain seemed dismayed but at a loss how to bring the man back to proper conduct. After the ranting had run on for a number of minutes, Eversole interrupted and asked that he be allowed to speak. It was with some difficulty that the captain quieted his sailor.

Eversole said judiciously, "It appears that part of the difficulty was due to language. When the boy was asking to end the match, the sailor failed to understand him. This being the case, it was naturally Mr. Kotovsky's duty to separate them."

"Perhaps so," Captain Kayahara said, "but it was not his duty to beat the sailor."

This was apparently what the sailor had charged during his tirade. Eversole avoided an argument on the point, merely pointing out that apparently everyone got excited. Then he added:

"Captain, I call to your attention a most serious fact. Your sailor did not report these events to you, the captain of the ship. Instead he went to his quarters and got a large knife and went onto a deck full of children with the purpose of using it. He was, in fact, taking over the discipline of this ship. This is something you must not tolerate!"

The captain frowned and studied the desk for a moment. He admitted it was a bad situation and said, "I have confiscated his knife and will not return it."

"That is not enough," Eversole snapped. "You must make your men understand that you are the master of this ship and that not one of them has the right to discipline any of the passengers on board by actions, force or words."

A nod of agreement came from the captain, and then a pause in the proceedings. The Americans conferred together in low voices. The captain showed no indication that he was going to discipline the sailor, who remained completely unabashed by the proceedings and continued to glower at them. If they demanded immediate and strong disciplinary action from the captain and he refused, his authority over the crew might be further undermined and the danger to the children increased. It seemed unwise to press the point until they were safely in New York.

Eversole strongly recommended to the captain that he instruct his crew to forget the entire incident, not even to talk about it. He would so instruct the children and the teachers and the American personnel. Further, he recommended that contact between crew and passengers be kept to the absolute minimum and on the most formal basis.

The captain nodded his agreement.

"I suggest finally," Eversole said, "that for your own protection against any future legal proceedings I have two of my physicians examine the sailor for any wounds or bruises."

"No," Captain Kayahara said, "that is not correct for you to do."

Eversole turned to Miss Domerschikoff and said, "Make the offer of medical examination directly to the sailor."

She did so and immediately the sailor launched into another angry tirade, shaking his fist at Kotovsky. He went on and on while the captain sat staring straight ahead, making no effort to silence him. Finally, with the sailor still shouting, the Red Cross people stood up and filed out of the saloon.

The dance was ordered ended at nine-thirty and by ten the decks were clear and all the children in their bunks. Since rumor and speculation raged through the ship, it was decided that the children should be given a frank, though limited, report of the events of the evening. In each hold a teacher told the hushed children that a sailor had pulled a knife on Ilin but that it had all been because of a misunderstanding due to the language barrier. To avoid any future misunderstandings the children must not bother the sailors, not try to play with them, not go into their areas of the ship. The sailors were busy men and had a lot of work to do and must be left absolutely alone so they could run the ship.

Every effort was made not to put the crew in a bad light, to smooth over the day's events. Some success was perhaps achieved with the smaller children, but little with the older ones and certainly none with the teachers. The Russian-Japanese hostility was an historic fact and the Americans might suppress it but they could not exorcise it, not aboard the *Yomei Maru*.

It dawned hot and still the next morning and the sea was without a ripple on its glassy surface except for the wake of the *Yomei Maru*. The heat intensified hour on hour and by ten o'clock the pale, scorching sun hung motionless in an aluminum sky. Eversole made the rounds of inspection that morning, as both Walker and Bramhall had been up all night and were sleeping. All the holds were in order, bunks made and decks swept, and no disciplinary problems reported. Ship life seemed routine, with the necessary work being done slowly and quietly. It was as if everyone was enervated, not just from the heat but from the excess of emotion of the night before.

The noon meal came and went, followed by an afternoon siesta. Eversole allowed himself a small amount of self-congratulation for having taken a firm stand with the captain. It had done the job.

At four in the afternoon he was walking along the starboard deck and saw the teacher Kotovsky sitting on a rope locker, reading a book. He thought to approach him and say a few pleasantries but before he could do so the sailor who had fought with Ilin appeared from behind a lifeboat and stopped before the teacher. He had a broom in his hand and he now shook it angrily in the teacher's face.

Kotovsky gestured for the sailor to go away and when he didn't, the teacher turned his head to look in another direction. This infuriated the sailor and he ran around to appear again and increased his threatening gestures.

"Stop that!" Eversole cried out, striding quickly toward them.

The sailor disappeared back around the lifeboat, throwing a villainous look over his shoulder as he went.

At this moment one of the older boys rushed up to Eversole from the other direction and blurted, "Burenin has been threatened by one of the crew." Burenin was one of the boys who had testified at the inquiry.

"Is Burenin hurt?" Eversole demanded sharply.

"The sailor didn't actually stab him, he just threatened like this." The boy drew his finger across his throat. "The sailors went away but we're afraid they'll be back tonight."

Eversole stood quite still for a moment, his face flushed with anger. Then he turned on his heels, went into his own cabin and shut the door.

Eversole was a physician, a Christian missionary, a pacifist by temperament and conviction. Anger was alien to him and now as he experienced it in such full and unaccustomed violence, he was ashamed. He spent ten minutes locked up alone and when he emerged he was white-faced but in full control of himself. He went directly to Captain Kayahara's cabin, walked in and remained standing while he spoke in cold and measured terms.

He reported the two latest developments and the captain seemed quite shaken by the news. Then Eversole said:

"If any member of your crew again draws a knife, or pretends to draw a knife, or makes any threatening statement or gesture, to the children or the Russian or American personnel, I shall require you to put into the nearest Panamanian or Cuban port where I shall take aboard a strong American military guard. The cost of diverting the ship and taking aboard the guard will be charged to the owners of this ship. I now return to my stateroom where I will put this in writing. You will have a copy forthwith."

In the following minutes there was a great hurrying and

scurrying aboard the *Yomei Maru* as the crew was summoned to a meeting in the fo'c'sle.

At five o'clock the captain came to Dr. Eversole's cabin and announced that he had been most stern with the crew and they had all promised there would be no more trouble. Eversole acknowledged the report with a thin-lipped nod of his head.

It seemed that the captain had finally been forced to firmness, but Eversole allowed himself no optimism. He would wait and watch developments, and at the first sign of a new crisis he would put into port for troops.

A crisis returned, but when it did it wore an entirely different aspect, and no military guard would be able to resolve it. It came by wireless, crackling into the radio shack during the early morning hours of Sunday, August 22.

NINETEEN

The wireless message was from the Washington, D.C., headquarters of the American Red Cross. After transcribing it, the radio operator delivered it to Bramhall, who read it with mounting unease. Robert Olds' arguments had carried the day—the Petrograd children would not be returned immediately to their homes but would be taken to France for another extended encampment.

The cable, signed by Riley Allen and Livingston Farrand, read: "Owing to the international situation also critical food situation Petrograd necessary land entire Colony France, repatriating thence by individuals or groups if possible. Red Cross making every effort early delivery children to parents. Present plans France necessitate retention entire American and Russian personnel in order to operate Colony along lines Russian Island. Authorize you announce the foregoing. Assure Colony stay in France merely preliminary to getting home. Emphasize impossibility direct entrance *Yomei Maru* Petrograd on account military international situation. Received your cable from Santa Cruz deeply regret heat stroke cases. Keep us closely advised about conditions of ship. Have good location

New York. Entertainment plans progressing. Warmest regards
all Colony. Farrand-Allen."

Bramhall took the message to Eversole and together they
discussed its possible impact upon the Colony. They agreed it
would be considerable. With the possible exception of Japan,
France was the least suitable country in the world to choose
for an encampment of Russian children. France was strongly
supporting Baron Piotr Wrangel's White Army which still held
out in the Crimea, and she was supplying and masterminding
the Poles' war against Russia in Central Europe. During this
very month the Poles were invading the Ukraine, with French
matériel and under tactical plans drawn by French General
Maxime Weygand.

The Petrograd Colony was not pro-Bolshevik, but where
Russian fought Pole or French or Japanese, they were certainly
pro-Russian. Their nationalism was intensified by the fact of
being adrift. Disoriented on so many things, having so little
control over their own fate, they clung all the more fiercely to
their identity as Russians.

"Well," Bramhall finally sighed, "I guess there's nothing for
it but to read this cable to the Colony."

"Perhaps I'd better add a few remarks," Eversole said, "to
try to soften its impact."

"You can try," Bramhall said.

That morning the entire Colony was gathered on deck and
the cable read. There was sober and rapt attention from everyone, even the smaller children sensing that something momentous was being said. When it was completed, Eversole stood
up and said:

"This cable should stamp on your minds several facts. First,
that the American people through the American Red Cross are
going to stand back of you until your government is in a position to receive you. Second, the American Red Cross is not a
government organization, it is not supported by the government. The Red Cross is an organization of the people of America, and supported by the people. Ninety percent of all the

money used by the Red Cross is given by the poor people of America. Owing to postwar conditions in America, living is very difficult and expensive and there is every reason why the people should wish to land you in Petrograd at the earliest possible moment, but they are willing to continue to share with you until you can safely return home. I am proud of the people of America for this unselfish spirit, and their determination to finish the project of your repatriation regardless of the sacrifices it costs them."

Eversole was asking for gratitude. He was asking for it at the wrong time and under the wrong conditions, and he didn't receive it. His little speech was received in silence, not a hostile silence but one of preoccupation. Every Russian man, woman and child was grappling with the stunning fact that they were not headed for home, as they had thought, but for a foreign and hated land. Homesickness, patriotism, frustration, fear— all these emotions boiled within them. There was no space for gratitude.

The meeting was dismissed and the Americans watched closely as the teachers and children returned to their various occupations. Some sort of protest, or even an outbreak of violence might be expected. It would probably come from the older boys, the Americans decided, and stern measures would have to be used to keep the peace. The relationship with the crew was already explosive, and even a minor infraction of the ship's routine could bring appalling consequences.

For the rest of that morning the *Yomei Maru* was a deceptively silent ship. There were many conversations but they were held in low tones and through tight lips and could not be heard above the slap of the waves against the steel bow.

The protest came that afternoon. There was no violence in it, but its very calmness made it the more formidable. P. V. DeGeorge sent word that a committee representing the teachers would like to meet with the Americans at four o'clock. When the committee arrived it consisted of DeGeorge, Nikolay Borsouk, Seraphina Victorova, Dr. Liperovsky and Madam

Zorn. When everyone had been seated, DeGeorge stood up to speak. His words were delivered calmly and carefully, only a slight quaver in his voice revealing the emotion that lay behind them. He said:

"It was over two years ago that we left Petrograd, promising the parents of the children that we would return them in three months. There have been good reasons why we have been unable to keep our promise, but we have always tried. At no time did we ever agree to anything that would delay the return of the children to their parents. We embarked the children on this ship under the promise that we would sail directly to Petrograd. Now we are told it is not to be done."

He paused a moment. He did not charge betrayal, but the unspoken word hung in the air.

"The children and the teachers feel unbounded gratitude to the American Red Cross," he continued, "but we cannot go to France. France is at war with our country. Our older boys would no doubt be pressed into military service. At the least we would be captives, hostages. Whatever the intentions of the American Red Cross, we do not believe you could stand against the French government once we were on French soil. At the best, this plan means an indefinite delay in our return home. To agree to such a thing would be to betray our trust."

He paused again, gathering himself for the final statement: "If the Red Cross persists in this plan, we teachers will walk off the ship in New York and take the children with us."

There was the gauntlet! It had been thrown not by a hot-headed adolescent, but by mature and responsible men and women.

The Americans sat silent and thoughtful. Were there any arguments that could sway these teachers? A look at the set, Russian faces indicated there were not. They were obviously prepared to carry out their threat, whatever the consequences. It had become a matter of principle, and was, therefore, not negotiable. It was up to the Americans to retreat, or else!

Wisely the Americans neither argued nor retreated. Eversole

said quietly, "We shall transmit your feelings and opinions to Washington for the most careful consideration."

The meeting was at an end.

Red Cross Chairman Farrand was shocked when he received Bramhall's detailed cable from the *Yomei Maru*. He had not been prepared, despite Riley Allen's warning, for the Colony's reaction. He wondered if Bramhall and Eversole had backed up the plan with enough vigor. The plan was a prudent one, and surely the teachers could be brought to realize that.

Farrand dispatched a cable to the *Yomei Maru* assuring the Colony that all decisions on future plans would be held in abeyance until they arrived in New York.

TWENTY

Riley Allen arrived in New York ten days ahead of the *Yomei Maru*. The local chapters of the Red Cross and Junior Red Cross had been hard at work on housing and entertainment plans, and they reported that considerable emotion would undoubtedly be generated by the children's visit. There were many Russian organizations in the city and each was demanding exclusive right to entertain the Colony. This intramural competition was sharpened by political and religious differences, and each group was inordinately sensitive to any appearance of Red Cross favoritism to a rival.

In contrast, the various government bureaus with whom Allen had to deal wanted the very minimum contact with the children. The Red scare abroad in the land made the bureaucrats tremble at the very mention of the word Russian. Some of Allen's troubles were revealed in an August 21 report sent to Keppel:

Today I went to see Commissioner-general of Immigration Caminetti to ask what detail of procedure would be necessary to arrange for entry into the United States of such children as might be claimed by relatives here able and willing to take them and with proof that their parents are not in Petrograd. I was considerably surprised to find that Mr. Caminetti was not acquainted with the plan of leaving such children in America, and after a short conversation it was evident that we shall have to have a decision from the department on this point. He seemed to feel hesitation about admitting any Russian children into America and stated that the whole matter would have to be placed before him in writing. I have accordingly written the attached letter, to be forwarded to him on Monday, if you approve. Mr. Caminetti stated that he does not wish to give this matter newspaper publicity and evidently is apprehensive that the proposal to admit the Russian children into the United States will occasion criticism.

As the government bureaus shied away from assisting the Red Cross, various political pressure groups began a campaign of propaganda in an effort to influence the ultimate disposition of the children. One of the first to open up was the Russian Soviet Bureau which, in the absence of diplomatic relations between Russia and the United States, acted as Lenin's unofficial spokesman in this country. The head of the Bureau was Mr. L. Martens and he sent a peremptory telegram to Frederick Keppel demanding to know when and under what circumstances the children would be returned to Petrograd. Keppel replied that Riley Allen would be in New York and would answer any of his questions.

On August 23, five days before the arrival of the *Yomei Maru,* Allen sent the following memorandum to Keppel:

I telephoned this morning to the Russian Soviet Bureau and stated to Mr. Martens that I was in town and if he had any question concerning the welfare of the Petrograd children, their stay in New York, etc., I should be glad to give him any information possible. He asked me if I could come to his office but I explained that I had a number of people coming to see me this morning, but would be at the Atlantic Division Office of the Red Cross all morning and ready to see anyone interested in the welfare of the children.

A short time later a young man appeared, introducing himself and giving me his card with the name of Mr. Kenneth Durant, saying that he was here for Mr. Martens. He talked for perhaps half an hour and I told him about how the Red Cross had undertaken the care of the children, our endeavors to return them overland, our inability to do so and our present undertaking to transport them by sea. I also told him that all factions of Russia at Vladivostok had cooperated in the arrangements of placing the Colony on board the *Yomei Maru* and that Mr. Vilensky, the Soviet representative of Vladivostok, was perfectly aware of our plans and had visited the colony at Russian Island. This was in response to a question from him if Mr. Vilensky were acquainted with this situation with reference to the Colony . . .

He then asked me as to the immediate plans for returning the children and I said that the steamer would stop at a French port and that from France we would endeavor to get in touch with the parents and return the children in groups or as individuals just as rapidly as possible. I explained that in France we could be assured of accommodations for the children, that it was our European Headquarters and that we felt the best interests of the Colony from the standpoint of housing, food and clothing, and the question of plans to return them to their parents could best be served by landing the Colony temporarily in France. I stated that there were indications that many of the parents are now outside of Soviet Russia and that under such circumstances it would not be advisable to try to take the entire Colony into Petrograd at once.

Mr. Durant said immediately that the proposal to land the children in France would be received with much resentment by Russians in New York and I assumed he meant by this the Russians whose sentiments are more or less represented by the Soviet Bureau. He said that France is regarded as the bitterest foe of Russia and that he feared the Petrograd children would not get home. We talked about this a great deal, and I said that the decision to land the children in France was entirely one relating to their welfare, solely from a Red Cross standpoint, and without any bearing on political or international issues, except as these issues made it impossible to land the children directly in Petrograd. I gathered, however, at the end of our conversation that he felt that there would undoubtedly be in New York much hostility to this plan of landing in France. . . .

The *Yomei Maru* crept through the Narrows and into the wide harbor of New York during the early hours of August 28. As it approached Manhattan the sun burned off the morning haze and the towered island stood bold and beautiful against the sky. It was a great spectacle for the children, but they were also one for the men who worked this busy harbor.

Unlovely to begin with, the *Yomei Maru* had not improved during her 10,105-mile voyage from Vladivostok. Her sides were streaked with rust and refuse, her superstructure needed painting, her brightwork needed polishing, her stays and lines needed tightening, her generally disheveled air spoke of an indifferent crew. All the more surprising, then, was her ring of bright young faces. Coast Guardsmen, Immigration and Public Health officials, deckhands on tugs and lighters and freighters, gentlemen aboard private yachts, commuters packed aboard the giant ferries, all who looked on these children were moved. The arrival of the *Yomei Maru* had been well-publicized in the press, everyone knew the history of the Colony, their rescue by the Red Cross, their wanderings across two continents and two oceans, and their presence gave the ship an air of adventure.

The harbor craft blew their horns and whistles in salute, the commuters waved from their ferries and fleetingly wished their own destinies were not a ferry trip up the bay to an office in the city, but aboard the romantic *Yomei Maru* to travel around the world.

At noon the ship docked at pier G in Jersey City. The first to debark was a stretcher case and the children gathered around with sober faces, for it held their favorite teacher, Maria Gorbochova. She had fallen sick during the passage through the Panama Canal and was now being taken to New York's Post-Graduate Hospital. The doctors had diagnosed her illness as mastoiditis, an infection of the bone behind her right ear, and told the children it was serious but not alarming and she would be cared for in one of the best hospitals in the world. Nevertheless, seeing their dearest friend being carried away helpless into a strange city made many of the children weep.

It was all done with dispatch, however, and there followed the bustle of the debarkation of the Colony and the prisoners of war. Immediately upon leaving the ship, they marched across the wide pier and reimbarked on three United States Army steamers which took them to Staten Island where they were to be quartered in the barracks of Fort Wadsworth.

Every bunk had been numbered to receive its occupant and by midafternoon the entire Colony had settled in. The physical layout of the fort was ideal for their purposes. The buildings were commodious, and they were equipped with showers and modern lavatories. The mess kitchen and dining rooms were ample and presided over by military personnel from the Cooks and Bakers School in Camp Meade, Maryland. The camp was surrounded by a fence and patrolled by military sentries.

The great advantage of the fort was that it afforded maximum control of the Colony. The children were isolated from the confusion and health dangers of the city, yet close enough to it for quick visits. It had not occurred to the Red Cross that they would soon be charged with keeping the children prisoners in an internment camp.

Now that the Colony had arrived, it was Allen's job to convince them that encampment in France would not materially delay their return to their parents. He met with his staff first, and he was frank about his misgivings over the plan, but the decision had been made by the Central Committee and he urged all of them to help reassure the Colony as to the Red Cross's basic intentions.

"Riley," Mother Campbell said, "there's been so much rumor and gossip going on that I think you should talk to the children yourself."

"I plan on doing so."

"And to the teachers," Eversole added.

"And to the teachers," Allen agreed.

He adjourned the meeting and went to the barracks to plead the case. This slight, soft-spoken man moved among the excitable Russians, speaking calmly and reassuringly. Such was the respect and affection they held for him that the defiant attitude the teachers had struck wilted away, and the fears that had haunted the children disappeared. Riley Allen was a transparent man. He loved them and wanted what was best for them. And they could see what was in him.

The first day at Fort Wadsworth passed without incident. The second day was Sunday and outdoor Orthodox services were held with singing by the choir from St. Nicholas' Cathedral. Following the services the children ran about the grounds full of happy animal spirits, suddenly freed from the confinement of shipboard life. But things were to change during the afternoon.

The scheduled entertainment was a pageant called "A Russian Market" and it was to be presented by a professional New York company of entertainers called the Russian Isba. The company arrived shortly after noon with their canvas sets and their props and instruments, and with them came New York Russians by the boatload. Each ferry that landed at Staten Island disgorged another hundred or so from the city and surrounding territory. They brought presents of candy and food and toys and they swarmed in through the gates of Fort Wadsworth and descended upon the children with glad cries and emotional Russian words. A few, a very few, were relatives; most were merely countrymen who had come to see the children from the land of their birth, or their parents' birth.

By two o'clock there were three thousand Russian visitors at the fort, and it became apparent that among them were a fairly large number of Reds or Red sympathizers. They could be spotted by the purposefulness with which they moved. They took the children off in small groups and talked to them with great seriousness. Others of them circulated among the teachers.

They were proclaiming what awaited the Colony in France.

The older boys would be pressed into military service and sent to the Polish front to fight against their own country; the older girls would be sent to brothels; the younger children would be held as hostages; the teachers would be imprisoned.

As these words were spread, faces grew long and a foreboding filled the camp. That night in the barracks there was much excited talk. The next day Riley Allen received from the Colony a hastily drawn document:

The American Red Cross. The boys and girls of the Petrograd Children's Colony PROTEST OVER THE SENDING OVER OF THE COLONY TO FRANCE.

We boys and girls of the Petrograd Children's Colony declare to the American Red Cross that we will not go to France. We cannot go to a country thanks to which the population of Russia died and is dying by the tens and hundreds of thousands from the consequence of the blockade; which is sending to Poland weapons of war that take to the graves hundreds of thousands of best Russian young forces.

We cannot live in a country where the Russian Soldiers who gave their blood during many years on the Western front for the interest of France, were shot or sent to hard labor in Africa. If the American Red Cross did not realize till now that between us is quite a big number of children who understand, we want by this protest to draw the attention of the American Red Cross to this fact and we demand that the American Red Cross should change its decision about the sending of the Colony to France and would send us to Petrograd.

We wait for the answer from the American Red Cross at noon, September 3rd, 1920.

It was not only a protest but an ultimatum!

Great consternation ran through the Americans and at a staff meeting called by Allen that morning there were some hot words.

"Riley, I'm simply outraged that they would do this to you!" one of the staff exclaimed.

"To *me?*" Allen said with mild surprise. "I do not see this as a personal attack."

"Well, what I mean is that it's unthinkable that you should have rescued these children, cared for them and fed them and loved them all these months, only to have them accept the words of a bunch of strangers against yours."

"Ah, but they weren't strangers," Allen said. "They were Russians. The children were listening to their own blood, and to their own language. And above all, they were hearing the words they wanted to hear—that they should go directly home. I should have been surprised if they responded in any other manner."

"That's all well and good," Bramhall said, "but we're faced with this ultimatum. What are we going to do about it?"

"First, we must understand what it is *not*. It is *not* an attack upon us. It may be an attack upon our policy, but not upon us. They still consider us their friends, mistaken friends to be sure, but friends nevertheless. We must exercise the greatest care not to alter that relationship. We must not be censorious, we must not deny them a right to express their opinions, we must keep reassuring them that our only goal is to return them to their parents."

"But what of the ultimatum?" Bramhall demanded.

"Oh, that's five days off," Allen said, grinning. "A lot can happen in five days."

That afternoon there was scheduled an official welcome from the City by Mayor John Hylan. A transit strike occupied the Mayor's time and he could not make it to the ceremonies on Staten Island, but he sent a message of greeting. There were similar messages from a dozen New York civic and fraternal organizations, many of them inviting the children to parties and entertainments and excursions. There was also a message officially purported to be from the President of the United States. This was at a time when Wilson lay ill and incommunicado in the White House. James Rule, national director of the Junior Red Cross, had asked presidential intimate Dr.

Stockton Axson to obtain appropriate greetings. The letter was forthcoming, and with a covering note from Axson:

THE WHITE HOUSE
Washington

24 August 1920

My dear Mr. Rule: I think you will understand that in the present circumstances, with the President's many burdens and limited strength, it is not always possible to rush through a matter. This has been attended to as expeditiously as possible.

I fear the President's letter is not in exactly the form you desired, but I did not like to ask him to change it, and I hope that it, especially in the last paragraph, will answer the purpose— the signed photographs and the message on the President's photograph will, I hope, answer the purpose nicely.

With warm regards, yours faithfully,
Stockton Axson

The letter was by no means in "the form" the Red Cross had hoped, but exactly how inappropriate to the situation was not realized until it was read to the Colony that day on Staten Island:

THE WHITE HOUSE
Washington, D.C.

24 August 1920

My dear Mr. Rule: Doctor Axson has shown to Mrs. Wilson and me your letter to him of August twenty-fourth, and I write to beg that you will convey to the colony of Petrogard children which has been in the care of the American Red Cross Commission to Siberia during the past year, and is now being transported by the Commission to Brest, France, our warmest greetings. I am sure that you may say to them that the hearts of all the people of the United States go out in the tenderest sympathy and that they will always hope that their future will be happy enough to make some amends for the past. Cordially and sincerely yours, Edith Bolling Wilson & Woodrow Wilson.

When the Colony heard the President of the United States say that they were on their way to France, they exchanged grim looks. That Wilson had in all probability never seen the letter and most certainly had not written it, were facts the children could not be expected to comprehend.

On that same day, while the Colony was being transported in city buses for a sight-seeing tour of Manhattan, the controversy broke out in the daily press. The *New York Tribune* ran a front page story headlined "Radicals Plot to Take Waifs from Red Cross." The drop head read "Bolshevik Agents Visit Fort Wadsworth and Seek to Stir Revolt Among 780 Russian Children . . . Alleged Plan Afoot to Distribute Youngsters from Siberia in This Country." The story recounted the events on Staten Island, and included a remarkable paragraph which read, "Following a day of agitation, conducted quietly among the children by Bolshevik agents, a group of about fifty Russian attendants accompanying the children met and formed a soviet last night. They elected a committee and decided to send it as a delegation to the authorities at the Fort to discuss plans for the continued journey of the refugees."

L. Martens kept up a drumfire of correspondence, writing the A.R.C. Headquarters on letterheads which would indicate the authority of his voice. The following was typical:

RUSSIAN SOCIALIST FEDERAL SOVIET REPUBLIC
Bureau of the Representative
in the United States of America

Address:
World's Tower Building
110 West 40th St.
New York

September 7th, 1920
No. A-15

Mr. Frederick P. Keppel,
Vice Chairman,
American Red Cross,
Washington, D.C.

Dear Sir:
I have received your letter of September 3rd and note with satisfaction that the American Red Cross is considering my protest against the taking of the 780 Russian children to France. I feel sure that upon careful deliberation you will decide against an action which would be an obvious injustice to the children and their parents.

I urge you, however, as soon as possible to make a public announcement that the children will not be sent to France and that they will be sent to their homes without delay. I know from reliable reports that the children are in a most unhappy state of dread lest they are to be sent to the unfriendly atmosphere of France, thus greatly delaying their homecoming and making them the innocent victims of international political enmity. A clear statement from you that it is not the purpose of the Red Cross to send them to France will relieve the fears of the children and make them better able to bear their impatient longings for their parents and their homes.

> *Yours very truly,*
> (Signed) L. Martens
> Representative of the Russian Socialist
> Federal Soviet Republic

The Russian language press in New York began to add fuel to the fire. Both *Novoye Russkoye Slovo* and *Russky Golos* printed verbatim copies of the protest the children had given to Riley Allen.

Editorially *Novoye Russkoye Slovo* declared:

The "Petrograd Colony," staying at present with us, is in a state of despondency. After two years of wanderings, after hard trials in the land of Kolchak and sufferings under Semenoff, they want to take the children to France . . . Why to France? . . . France that kept our war prisoners in such a state, locking them in African forts, put them on the same footing as the blacks, sending them against their will to the White guards and shooting them if they refused to go? There is no place for Russian children in France, the country that is provoking hate between Russia and Poland, that is sending munitions, that will kill Russian peasants and laborers, who may be fathers and brothers of the children we have now with us . . . Don't play politics with these children. It is enough to exhibit them—take them home.

The paper ended the editorial with a petition to be clipped and signed by the readers, a petition to the Red Cross demanding that the children be sent immediately to Petrograd.

Each day the attacks became more violent. By Wednesday,

one of the papers cried, "The sending of the children of the
Petrograd colony to France is monstrous . . . From the very
moment the children became wards and prisoners of the American Red Cross, their life became one long, demoralizing and
pointless trek. Why should our children and their teachers be
treated as convicts and be kept under military guard. And
what has the American Red Cross done with the teachers? It
has completely destroyed their authority and nullified their
pedagogical efforts. Those who rebelled were thrown out; the
rest just live in terrible moral squalor . . . The activities of the
American Red Cross vis-à-vis the Petrograd colony are in reality a combination of the most inhuman tortures inflicted on
hundreds of human beings."

The result of the newspaper controversy was to make *any*
action the Red Cross might take seem politically motivated. If
they persisted in sending the children to France they were
acting as agents of the French imperialists and sending young
boys to battle with their own parents. If they did not send
them to France they were knuckling under to the Bolsheviks
and sending innocent children to squalor and starvation in a
godless country. All but lost from view was the Red Cross's
basic and unaltered commitment that they would return the
children to their parents wherever those parents might be.

While passionate words were being printed and shouted,
Riley Allen quietly went his way in an effort to solve the
riddle. He began calling on representatives of the White Russian colony in New York, on the Orthodox religious groups, on
the representatives of the various foreign nations involved, and
to everyone he explained that while the children might be
wrong in their fear of military service in France, their feelings
were quite sincere and not at all evidence of their embracing
Bolshevism.

He was surprised to find that the White Russians by and
large agreed with the Reds on the question of France and were
not at all in favor of taking the Colony there.

Allen entered in the ship's log, which he had resumed keeping: "We next went to the office of Mr. Bakhmetff, who appears as the Russian (White) Ambassador and who claims to be the legal successor of the Russian Ambassador of the old days of the Czaristic and Kerensky governments. Mr. Bakhmetff, while absolutely anti-Bolshevik, said he could understand the feeling of the children against going to France and had much the same viewpoint himself."

Unfortunately the White Russians' solution to the problem was not very realistic. They proposed that the children be kept in America and given out for adoption among the White Russian colony.

Allen now conceived an alternate plan. If the Red Cross insisted on a European delay before returning the children to their parents, it might be feasible to place the Colony in a camp in England rather than France. He approached the French chargé d'affaires. His account of this meeting was entered in the log:

"With this plan in mind we called on the French chargé d'affaires to explain the situation to him, and especially that he might suggest to the British representative the advisability of taking up with the British government a temporary halt of the children at an English port. We found the French chargé distinctly unsympathetic and with an inclination to be rather cynically humorous. He said that the whole affair was nothing more than an outburst of temper on the part of the children who ought to be spanked and put on the boat anyway . . ."

Allen seemed to have come to a dead end.

TWENTY-ONE

While the propaganda barrage thundered, while the Whites and the Reds struggled for the children's bodies and souls, the children went sight-seeing and became the darlings of New York.

The city was moved by the poignancy of their migration, enchanted by their blond handsomeness and good manners, delighted at their innocent excitement and open admiration for everything American. Gifts of every kind flooded into Fort Wadsworth, along with every conceivable sort of invitation for entertainment.

One of the highlights of the week was a steamer trip up the Hudson River to visit West Point. The cadets paraded for them, and they sang and danced for the cadets. It was a gala day for both soldier and moppet.

However, the long shadow of the controversy began to reach out for them in their public appearances. It intruded in an ugly and unexpected way on Friday, September 3. They were scheduled to make a well-publicized visit to the Bronx Zoo. A fleet of buses picked them up at the fort, took them to the ferries, across the bay to Manhattan, and uptown to the zoo in the Bronx. In the Bronx and nearby Queens there were large colonies of White Russians and they were out in force to see the children. As usual, they brought with them many gifts, mostly bags of candy and fruit.

When the children came pouring out of the buses the Russian adults sent up a cheer and called out greetings. The children laughed and shouted back. Gifts were now proffered and the children began to accept them with words of thanks.

Suddenly a dozen men appeared and began to intervene between the children and the adults, and with shouts and gestures indicated that no gifts could be passed to the children until they had first inspected them. It was not an order easily enforced in the confusion and these soberly dressed, impassive-looking men went around snatching bags out of the children's hands and peering into them. Usually they found grapes or peaches. Slowly the men were able to herd the children away from the adults and establish a cordon sanitaire between the two groups.

Burle Bramhall was in charge of this outing and he stormed up to one of these men and demanded, "Just what do you think you're doing? Who are you?"

The man removed a small leather wallet and flipped it open to reveal his identification card. He was an agent of the Division of Investigation, United States Department of Justice. Fourteen years in the future the name of his division would be changed to the Federal Bureau of Investigation.

"What are you doing here?" Bramhall demanded of the agent.

"There are to be no presents given the children that are not first examined."

"That's ridiculous. These people are only giving them candy and food and toys."

"Sorry," the man said politely, but there was really no note of apology in his voice. He added, "There must be no fraternization between the children and these people."

"By whose orders?" Bramhall demanded.

This time there was no answer at all, for the Justice Department agent dashed away to intervene between an eight-year-old girl and a bag of gumdrops.

Baffled and frustrated, Bramhall turned back to his charges and urged them on down the path toward the penned animals. The children began to move slowly, silently. The fun had gone out of the day. No one knew what these men might do next. Perhaps put them in jail?

The adults followed along behind, the happiness of giving soured within them. The Justice Department men displayed no expression beyond alertness to duty.

At lunchtime they all marched down to the restaurant in the middle of the zoo. The Colony had brought their own sandwiches, but the restaurant was to provide soup and milk. There was an area back of the restaurant enclosed by a high woven wire fence and it was here the children were led to eat. There had been nothing significant about the choice of the area, but under these circumstances it suddenly appeared so. The adults gathered angrily around the outside of the fence, shouting charges that the children were being imprisoned. Men shook their fists and shouted, women wept and shouted, the children became alarmed. The Justice Department men became tense under the barrage of abuse in an unknown language.

A riot was in the making, and Bramhall decided to end the zoo visit at once. He shouted orders for everyone to get back on the buses. The young children obeyed quickly enough but the older children were engaged in shouted dialogue with their compatriots.

"Vera! Vera Muraviova!" Bramhall shouted to an eighteen-year-old girl, the leader of about 160 Girl Scouts in the unit. "Line up your Scouts and march them to the buses."

The girl responded quickly and energetically, moving through the milling children with crisply shouted orders. Her Scouts responded, lined up and marched off to the buses. Now there remained the older boys, many of whom were as excited and angry as the adults. Bramhall moved among them, pleading, cajoling, ordering. But he'd no sooner get a group moving toward the buses when part of them would break away and run back to the fence to talk to the adults. Most alarming of all, the Justice Department men showed signs of moving in to enforce his orders. Theirs was the last assistance he wanted in these circumstances.

Then Bramhall spotted Vasili Vegronoon and called to him. Vasili was eighteen years old and one of the leaders of the older boys. He had been a champion swimmer back in Petrograd and commanded respect and some degree of hero worship.

"Vasili, you've got to help me."

"Yes, sir," Vasili said, but looked dubious.

"We've got to get the boys on the bus . . . at once!"

"They don't want to go," Vasili said. "They don't like being treated as if prisoners."

"I don't like the way things have been going here either, but I want us all out of it. Vasili, you know me well. Have I ever wanted anything that was not the best for you boys?"

Bramhall had been giving him English lessons over the past year and the boy did know him well.

"You always do what is right," Vasili agreed.

"Then I'm telling you it is right that we get everyone on the bus. And at once. Now let's get the job done."

Man and boy moved in together, and together they got the job done. In five minutes the last of the boys had mounted the steps of the bus, and the caravan moved off. The outing which had started with such happy laughter had ended just short of catastrophe.

When Bramhall reported back to Allen that afternoon they both speculated on what these events boded for the future. They were to learn almost at once for a phone call came from the New York Police Commissioner, Richard Enright, saying that he would like to send his deputy chief inspector to sit with Allen that evening and discuss "matters of mutual concern."

Present at the meeting the night of September 3 were Allen,

Red Cross train, full of medicines and clothing, prepares to leave Vladivostok in search of the "wild children."

Bolshevik guerrillas sabotage the Trans-Siberian Railway at Lake Baikal, delaying Red Cross rescue trains.

The "wild children" are found in the Urals.

Bramhall, Eversole, the inspector and the New York resident agent in charge of the Justice Department's Division of Investigation. The police officers had come to request that the Red Cross cancel the public festivities scheduled for the following day.

The climax of the entire visit was planned for this day. It was to be a gala reception and entertainment for the children in Madison Square Garden, and for weeks the New York Russians had been in a fever of preparation, rehearsing musicians and dancers and church choirs, writing speeches, buying gifts. The police were demanding that the Red Cross deny them this tribute.

"Why?" Allen demanded.

"It will give the Bolsheviks an opportunity for propaganda," the Justice Department agent said.

"This affair has the support of all the various Russian groups in New York," Allen replied. "There are supporters of the Czar, of Kerensky on the program committee, as well as supporters of Lenin. They've all agreed to make this a nonpolitical program of entertainment for these children. The choir of an Orthodox church will sing, the Russian Symphony will play, and our children will perform some folk dances and our balalaika orchestra will play."

"There'll be speeches," the inspector said challengingly.

"Just one. A welcoming speech by Mr. Brailowsky."

"Alexander Brailowsky is a Red sympathizer," the Justice Department man announced.

"I don't know about his politics," Allen said, "but he has submitted a copy of his speech to Mr. Burrell of our New York Chapter, and it was found to contain nothing political nor offensive."

The argument went back and forth for some time, and finally Allen said, "A great many people have invested a lot of time and energy in preparing this program. It would be a shame to disappoint them needlessly and I just don't see how we would be justified in doing so. As far as I am concerned, gentlemen, the program will continue. If either of you wish to cancel it for reasons of public safety, or whatever reasons may seem appropriate to you, you may do so. But it must be your responsibility."

Neither gentleman was ready to accept such responsibility.

By ten the following morning the line had begun to form outside the closed doors of Madison Square Garden. The event was not to take place until two-thirty that afternoon, but these were patient people and many had brought lunches of black bread and cheese wrapped in brown paper. The lines grew steadily and before the Garden doors opened at noon they extended around the block, and the soft, liquid murmur of Russian words filled the normally flavorless air. All classes of people had come for this event. There were broad and stolid-faced peasants wearing babushkas, delicate-featured intellectuals, the closed faces of political zealots, the haughty faces of aristocrats; there were Russians and Ukrainians and Armenians and Georgians and Moldavians; there were Christians and Moslems and Jews and agnostics and atheists. Nostalgia had brought this diverse crowd to one spot, an aching need to see themselves as they had once been—children of the motherland.

Shortly after two-thirty, a fleet of buses drew up in front of the Garden and the children, all scrubbed and starched, poured out of them and lined up. Under the proud escort of their teachers and Red Cross officials, they moved into the building. As they appeared on the floor of the vast auditorium and began to march down the center aisle, 16,000 throats roared. The children faltered, stunned by the sight and the sound. They looked but saw no individual face. The multiplication of one human voice by many thousands had worked a metamorphosis, created a many-celled monster that rose in ordered, protoplasmic tiers, up and up, to be finally lost in the gloom of the ceiling. And the sound it made was an animal sound, an echoing, guttural sound that issued from every cell of the vast body. It was difficult to tell what the sound meant, whether the animal felt pain or joy. In truth, it felt both.

After their initial disorientation, the children went on down the aisle to the block of seats reserved for them in front of the raised platform. The crowd slowly quieted, but remained alert, watchful for any excuse to express again its emotion.

The orchestra opened with excerpts from the works of Borodin. The composer had created a musical tapestry of Russian life, giving voice to all its contradictory extremes, telling of the nobility and the cruelty, the beauty and the harshness, the love and the hate. When the music ended the audience both wept and cheered.

Into this highly charged atmosphere stepped Alex Brailowsky to make his speech of welcome. There was no grace to the man or to his manner of speaking. His words were Russian and not immediately understandable to most of the Red Cross people, but his sentences were spoken in a staccato, harshly accented rhythm. Each sentence was a declamation.

Riley Allen suspected almost at once that this was a political polemic and not the speech that had been submitted to the Red Cross. The audience was beginning to respond to it. Suddenly a man jumped up in the balcony and shouted at Brailowsky, shaking his fist. Immediately two other men shouted down the first and the police moved in quickly to prevent a fight. Cheers and boos began to punctuate the speech, but the speaker paid no attention to either, plunging ahead with no slack in his rhythm.

"The Red Cross poses as a humanitarian organization," his strident voice echoed throughout the vast rotunda. "It pretends to be free and independent of the imperialist American government. But it is not humanitarian and it is not free. Its actions are the will of the American State Department. Its motives are political. The politics of Wall Street!"

Organized cheers came from a small group, followed by a scattering of boos.

"These poor children were captured by the Red Cross under

the transparent excuse that because they were of 'educated parents' their lives were threatened by the new and just socialist workers' and peasants' government. Against their will they were dragged across Siberia and placed in prison camps in Vladivostok. Against their will they were loaded on a cattle boat and shipped to America where they are displayed like so many freaks. Against their will they are about to be shipped by the imperialist warmongers to France, the enemy of Russia."

This produced a great outburst of cheers and boos.

"All the time the Red Cross proclaims its humanitarian motives, proclaims its anxiety for the fate of several hundred children, even delaying returning them home to Petrograd because of the supposed starvation that is raging there. What is the truth behind this sanctimonious falsehood? The Red Cross cares nothing for the lives of these children, else it would not tolerate a blockade of Russia which is resulting in the deaths of thousands of children!"

An emotional roar welled up from the audience. Several fights broke out but were quickly subdued by the police.

"In the Red Cross the voice of humanity is stifled by political motives . . . the politics of war and capitalism."

Brailowsky's speech abruptly ended, and into his place stepped Martens, the self-styled Soviet Ambassador. He took up Brailowsky's thesis but he was not harsh and pedantic in his delivery, he was a spellbinder, he wove his theme with skill, ornamented it with subtle innuendos, built to thundering climaxes. He had the audience whipped into an almost continuous roar for and against him, for and against the Red Cross, France, Russia, America. The audience became fragmented into many factions, each building its own store of fear and hate.

The children paled and stared apprehensively first at the speaker and then the howling audience. The police fingered their nightsticks nervously.

"For two long years these children have been exploited by the Red Cross," Martens cried passionately. "They have been underfed, they have been clothed in castoffs, they have been forced to labor for slave wages. Now they are to be disposed of by this 'humanitarian' organization. They are to be sent to France. And why? So that the boys, the manly hope for the survival of our motherland, will become cannon fodder on the Polish front. So that the girls, upon whose motherhood the very future of Russia depends, will be sent to brothels and destroyed."

His words were almost drowned by the crowd's roar. He raised his arms and pointed at the children and shouted with controlled hysteria, "Look down there. Look at the police surround them. Why? To protect them from us? They are blood of our blood. Flesh of our flesh. It is we who love them. No, the police are there because our children are captives of the Red Cross . . . they are hostages in the criminal conspiracy to smash the Motherland!"

Riley Allen's knowledge of Russian was not good enough for him to understand fully all the words being spoken but he understood the mood, and he could see the effect upon the audience. With some chagrin he recalled his meeting of the night before with the Justice Department agent and the New York police inspector. They had been right and he wrong. He had expected Brailowsky to keep his word, and his failure correctly to assess a man could now have terrible consequences.

The passions of the crowd were mounting and a massive clash between the Reds and the Whites seemed imminent. In the resulting riot what would happen to the children? Perhaps he should march them out of the auditorium right now. It would certainly require a police escort to get them through the crowd to the exits, and would that not seem proof of Martens' charges that the police were present only to keep the children captives of the Red Cross? And might not this lead to a mob effort to separate the children from the police?

Where did safety lie? Perhaps he should leave the children right where they were until the meeting had run its course. But this meant exposing them to all the poison being poured down upon them by the speakers. It was clear that the prepared program had been discarded and nothing would be heard but the most rabid sort of anti-American and anti-Red Cross propaganda. And the children were listening to every word with open mouths and wide eyes.

Whereas Riley Allen understood only the general mood of the speeches, Mother Campbell understood every searing word and she began to weep. What set off her tears were the remarks about the shabby appearance of the children. She and the nurses and teachers had worked so hard to clean them and dress them for this occasion, and she had been so proud of their appearance when they marched in. Making shame of their appearance seemed to her at this moment the most wounding thing that could be done. But as she listened to the calumny that continued from Martens her tears of pain turned to those of anger. She thrashed about in her chair, muttering to herself, denying each charge in choked, half sentences.

Martens finished his speech and his place was taken by another agitator. As Martens moved toward the back of the platform Hannah Brain Campbell came out of her chair. The act was the result of no conscious will, it was levitation by rage. She made her way blindly through the crowd and when she caught up with Martens she grabbed him by the arm to swing him around to face her. Then she let him have it, in Russian, nose to nose!

"You're a skunk and a liar!" she shouted. "Nothing but lies out there on the stage. You're a no-good bum and a liar! Why do you do it? We love those children, we care for them. Why you do say lies about us? Why do you say they look shabby?"

Martens tried to fend off her outburst. He retreated a step, shrugged his shoulders and said, "Compared to American children they look like tramps."

"Compared to the children we left behind in Vladivostok they look like royalty," she cried.

Their argument was causing a stir and several reporters

rushed up. One of them plucked at her sleeve and said, "Who are you? What's your name? What are you saying to him?"

"Leave me alone," she barked at the reporters. "I'm busy telling this rat what a skunk he is."

Martens, in an effort to pacify her, spread his hands and smiled and said, "Don't get so upset, lady, it's all propaganda on both sides."

"Propaganda!" she cried, aghast. "You tell lies that you know are lies, just to make propaganda? You don't care what happens to the children, you just make propaganda?"

She raised her two arms in the air. It was a gesture of appeal to the Lord to witness this infamy, but once they were up, they seemed poised to come down on Martens' head.

"Mother Campbell!" came a voice behind her. "What in God's name are you doing?"

She turned to face Riley Allen. "I'm just telling this skunk . . ."

"You're about to start a riot," he said sharply. "Come back at once. We need you with the children."

She hesitated. Just one good sock on the nose, she begged of herself, just *one!* But with a heavy sigh she turned to follow Allen. He was saying to her, "The children are becoming very excited and nervous, especially the younger ones. We've got to send some of the older boys and girls down among them to calm them."

As they rounded the edge of the speakers' platform and came into view of the children, Mother Campbell exclaimed, "Riley, look!"

One of the older boys in the Colony had just been introduced and was now making his way to the platform to speak. This was not part of the official program, it was obviously a surprise stratagem prepared by Martens and Brailowsky. Had they coached the boy to endorse their inflammatory words, give them the stamp of truth? If he did—Allen's mind reeled at the prospect. He began to feel alarm for the physical safety of his Red Cross people.

Allen strained forward to get a look at the boy now about to mount the platform steps. He was one of the older ones, eighteen or nineteen, and though Allen couldn't remember his name, he recognized him. He had been a member of the first Colony committee formed to protest the landing in France. As he now made his way forward on the speakers' platform, his young face set and white, applause and cheers greeted him. It went on for several minutes and Martens and Brailowsky moved up beside him to bask in the sound. At last it ended and as the boy prepared to speak there was silence, the first utter silence of the afternoon.

"We do not want to go to France," he said. "We want to go home to our parents whom we haven't seen in almost three years. We are Russians and we want to go home to Russia."

A sound went through the crowd. It was a sigh, a wave breaking on a shore, a small wave that ran ahead of the big breakers yet to come.

"We want to go home," the boy repeated, "and the Red Cross has said they would take us home. And we trust them."

Had he said *trust?* Or had the word been *mistrust?* Sixteen thousand pairs of ears strained to hear.

"We trust the American Red Cross because of what they have done for us," the boy continued. "We were starving in the Ural Mountains when they found us. They fed us and clothed us and let our teachers teach us. And they always promised they would return us to our parents. And we believe them. We would not be alive and here today but for the American Red Cross."

Abruptly, awkwardly, he ended his speech and walked off the stage. There was applause from the audience, but it was tentative. There had been such an abrupt change in mood, such reversal of words and facts, that the audience seemed uncertain what had happened exactly.

At this moment a sixteen-year-old girl, near hysteria, jumped up from her chair and rushed up on the platform. Brailowsky looked at her in surprise but made no move to stop her.

In a choked but penetrating voice she cried, "We did not know such awful things were going to be said about the Red Cross. They have been good to us. They love us. And we love them." She dissolved in tears and ran stumbling from the stage.

Riley Allen moved quickly. He jumped up on the platform, grabbed Brailowsky by the arm and said, "The children are now leaving. Please request the audience to remain seated until they are all out of the building." Brailowsky did as he was told.

The children stood, formed in twos, and began the long march up the middle aisle toward the exit. Applause began, then mounted to thunderous tones. And it was not just for the children, it was also in tribute to the Americans who marched proudly at their sides.

TWENTY-TWO

It was an emotional bus trip back to Fort Wadsworth that afternoon. Children by the dozens clustered around every Red Cross official to apologize tearfully for what had been said at the Garden and to proclaim their trust. By the time the Colony was finally bedded down that night everyone was in a state of exhaustion from the excesses of the day.

Expressions of gratitude and trust did not mean any lessening of the Colony's resistance to France, however. On the following day a stiff, anti-French resolution was passed by an "Executive Committee" elected jointly by children and teachers. The resolution thanked the Red Cross for its care and in the warmest terms, but it also contained the following words:

". . . Realizing that no obstacles should ordinarily lie in the way of a Red Cross organization to get into communication with even a belligerent government, we cannot conceive of any reasons why a ship flying a Red Cross flag should not sail directly for the port of Petrograd which is our home city."

This resolution was accompanied by a disquieting development in the camp. Groups of the older boys were beginning to ignore the rules and escape from the fort for trips into

Manhattan. Sometimes they were gone a day, sight-seeing and shopping, and sometimes two days. Upon return they were usually sullen in the face of any reprimand and demanded their "rights" to visit when and where they liked.

Implicit in their actions was the threat that if the Red Cross did not promise to give up the encampment in France, they would disappear into Manhattan for good.

Opposition to France came from another and unexpected quarter. Allen learned of it when Mother Campbell marched into his office and said, "Riley, I'm so darn mad!"

He grinned. "Seems to me you've been mad a fair share of the time lately, Mother Campbell."

She couldn't help returning his grin. "Maybe I'm getting crotchety, but I just don't like some of the things that been happening."

"Well, there might be some room for improvement here and there," Allen agreed judiciously. "Just which area did you have in mind?"

"The prisoners of war have struck," she exclaimed.

"They have . . . what?"

"They have struck and walked off the *Yomei Maru.*"

Allen passed his hand briefly over his eyes and then said, "Give it to me from the beginning."

"Well, this morning I loaded them all on a tug and took them over to the ship in Jersey to get her cleaned up to receive the children. That ship is a mess, Riley, just terrible. Well, I break out the mops and send them down in the holds. After a time I hear some mutterings down there and then up they come and announce they're quitting. They say they won't sail with the ship unless we promise not to go to France."

"Ah," said Allen.

"They say that they are afraid the French will intern them in prison camps. I told them the Red Cross wouldn't let that happen to them but they don't think we'd be strong enough to protect them once on French soil. I got so darn mad at them and I told them how ungrateful they were acting, after all we had done for them."

"But that didn't change their minds," Allen observed.

"No, it didn't. I'd like to hire replacements and turn them loose right here in New York."

"I'm afraid the Immigration Department would take a dim view of that. I pledged my word that the P.O.W.'s would not leave the ship or Fort Wadsworth."

"It would serve them right if we sent them back to Vladivostok."

"We don't have the money for that. And if we did, I'm not sure the punishment would fit the crime."

"They're practically guilty of mutiny!"

Allen shook his head. "They're guilty of being afraid. Just as the children are afraid to go to France."

"Riley, what's going to happen?"

"One thing is clear. If we follow our present policy, if we insist on a French encampment, we can only get the Colony there by force. And any Red Cross undertaking that requires force . . ." he spread his hands.

"What can we do?"

"Mother Campbell, if we have a wrong policy there is only one thing we can do—change it to a right one."

"But Washington. . . ."

A frown of annoyance passed briefly over Allen's face, but then he laughed. "It's been my experience that Washington sometimes makes it difficult to see the woods for the trees. I have asked Keppel to come here to New York to review the situation with me. He's arriving this afternoon."

Allen had been sending daily reports to Washington, and when Frederick Keppel arrived he was not ignorant of the developing crisis, but he was hardly prepared for what was to happen on September 9. But no one was prepared for that. One of the children was killed by a member of the armed guard at Fort Wadsworth.

Private Jack Berhim was of Russian ancestry, a naturalized American citizen, for three months a member of the United States Army, and member of Company "K," 22nd Infantry, assigned to guard duty while the children occupied the bar-

racks at Fort Wadsworth. He spoke Russian, had a sunny disposition and loved to play with the children. He was a great
favorite in the camp.

He was relieved from guard duty at about seven-fifteen of
the morning of September 9, whereupon he slung his rifle over
his shoulder and started toward his own quarters. There was a
shell in the chamber of the rifle, for Berhim was a conscien-
tious young soldier and ready to repel any invasion of un-
authorized persons.

As he rounded a corner of one of the barracks occupied by
the older boys, fifteen-year-old Pavel Nikolaeff jumped out at
him. They were friends. Pavel carried a broom which he now
used smartly to present arms. Private Berhim snapped to attention and presented arms with his gun. It discharged and Pavel
fell dead with a bullet in his head.

It was a tragic accident, but when news of the event reached
the New York radicals they would most certainly try to make it
into something else. They would charge that the boy was shot
while trying to escape from his Red Cross imprisonment. In an
effort to forestall this, Allen requested that the military commander convene a court of inquiry at once, that day. On the
court was a captain, two lieutenants and three representatives
of the Red Cross, Drs. H. M. Coulter, L. Y. Ruega and Hal
Davison. There were a dozen witnesses, and all of them told
the same story and the court returned its verdict of accidental
death.

This verdict would not, of course, stop the Bolshevik cry of
"whitewash," but then something did happen to stop it. A
statement was prepared by the boys who saw the accident. It
read:

Statement Given by Boys Who Saw Accident: P. Nikolaeff
with a stick in his hand was demonstrating to the American
soldier the military methods. The soldier began to demonstrate
too and when he was raising the rifle to his shoulder it suddenly went off. The soldier did not expect this. Then they tell
that he was looking for a bandage but could not find it. Some
say that he wished to stab himself but he could not pull out his

bayonet as he was very much excited; he ran to the office and he exclaimed "Kill me" as the interpreter translated it to them. All boys who knew the soldier say that he was always very good to them and that he always used to play with them. All boys feel sure that the soldier did this without any intention and this happened quite accidentally. All boys of the eight barracks agree with this. Signed for All Boys, V. Zouev. I herewith confirm that this is a correct translation of the statement of eye witnesses of the above incident. M. Pazlozskaya.

For the second time the children had undercut the propaganda efforts of the Bolshevik sympathizers. They had done it for no reason of politics, for no ulterior motive, but simply because they possessed a child's view of the truth.

That night, after a long and emotionally exhausting day with the court of inquiry, Allen and Keppel sat down to take a hard look at Red Cross policy. It was obviously a shambles, and under increasing pressure from all sides. Keppel had with him a letter from the Association "Unity of Russia," an anti-Bolshevik organization. He passed the letter to Allen who read:

ASSOCIATION "UNITY OF RUSSIA"
37 West 84th Street
New York City.

Sept. 8, 1920.
Chairman, B. L. Brasel
Vice Chairman, J. J. Sikorsky
Treasurer, S. D. Zavarotiuk
Member of the Executive
Committee, J. A. Gotza
Secretary, V. M. Shumsky

F. P. Keppel, Esq.,
American Red Cross,
National Headquarters,
Washington, D.C.

Dear Sir:

The grave scandal which took place in connection with the sojourn of the 800 Russian children refugees from Soviet Russia, who are in this country in care of the American Red Cross, has now become a matter of public discussion.

The Russian elements in New York watched with deep regret the gradual but deliberate surrendering of these children by the American Red Cross to the Jewish East Side organizations which, naturally, are in full sympathy with their brethren, at present in control of Soviet Russia.

The Russian elements made various and repeated attempts to prevent a public scandal by means of extending their care to the Russian children. Ladies, belonging to the Russian community, have expressed their sincere willingness to help the American Red Cross in its endeavor to entertain these refugees in an orderly, decent and Christian manner. Unfortunately, however, the American Red Cross preferred to have the cooperation of Bolshevist men and women, with the result that the entertainment was immediately converted by these Jews and Jewesses into a public corruption of the innocent ones.

The undersigned, who was unanimously instructed by the members of the Association "Unity of Russia" to address these lines, personally witnessed the disgraceful propaganda which was carried out under the auspices and the banner of the Red Cross among these Russian children. You are probably informed about the series of scandalous happenings at the Zoological Garden, at Fort Wadsworth, and at Madison Square Garden. You must have heard how Brailowsky and several other anarchists, including Martens, urged the Russian children to protest against the wise decision of the American Red Cross to take the Russian refugees over to France. You probably are also aware that Bolshevist and anarchist leaflets, pictures of Trotsky, Joffe, Apfelbaum and other Bolshevist leaders, were distributed among the children, and red flags were given by Bolshevist women to the children between the ages of seven and ten.

The series of scandals was terminated by the recent escape of one hundred Russian children from Fort Wadsworth, which has been reported in the daily press.

Those who have watched the situation since the very first days of the arrival of the Russian party, knew in advance that a thing of this kind would happen, but they were unfortunately handicapped by the passive attitude on the part of the American Red Cross. Soap box agitators and political babblers took occasion to spread their propaganda which obviously is to the detriment both of this country and of Russia herself.

The Association "Unity of Russia," which is closely watching the developments of this situation, understands that Martens and his Bolshevist colleagues are urging the American Red Cross to send the Russian children to Soviet Russia. In fact, Mr. Martens, in Madison Square Garden, boasted that he had received instructions from Soviet officials on the other side of the water to have the

Russian refugees sent to Petrograd. We do not know the attitude of the American Red Cross to this disgraceful demand. We deem it our duty, however, to advise you that the sending of these children to Petrograd would be equal to murdering them. The deplorable sanitary conditions in Petrograd, combined with the acute lack of food, make this proposition impossible. We earnestly hope that the American Red Cross, after the sad experience which it had with the Bolshevist elements, will now listen to our sound and friendly warning and will flatly reject in the future cooperation with these professional trouble makers, and will also emphatically reject the very attempt to have the Russian children sent to Soviet Russia, thus preventing them from wholesale starvation and unspeakable tortures.

A copy of this letter is simultaneously being sent to the Department of State.

The Association "Unity of Russia" will appreciate very much a prompt answer to the above.

> *I am, dear Sir,*
> *Yours very truly,*
> (Signed) B. Brasel, Chairman
> Association "Unity of Russia"

The anti-Semitic tone of the letter revealed some of the baser passions that were being roused on all sides. Clearly the Red Cross had to move quickly and with firmness of purpose. Allen and Keppel talked late into the night and in the end they reached agreement on all steps: 1. The encampment in France would have to be abandoned. 2. It would be unwise to sail directly into Petrograd. 3. The *Yomei Maru* should sail for a neutral Baltic port.

Keppel sent a cable to Olds informing him of the change in plan, and followed it by a letter:

Sept. 9, 1920.

R. E. Olds, Esq.
American Red Cross,
4 Rue de Chevreuse,
Paris, France.

Dear Col. Olds:

After forty-eight hours of acute worry, I sent you the cable which I enclose herewith. It would have been impossible to give you an adequate picture of the situation here by cable and it will be hard enough by a letter, but I have no hesitation in saying that if you and Dr. Farrand had been in New York the past week, you would have reached the same conclusions that Riley Allen and Mr. Rogers, Manager of the Atlantic Division, and I myself reached as to the necessity of assuring the Petrograd Colony that its members would not be disembarked in France against their will.

I hope I have already made clear that the unanimous protest on the part of the adults and the more mature children took place immediately upon receipt of the wireless message notifying them that the preliminary disembarkation would take place in France, and of course before any influence could be brought to bear upon the Colony by the Russians in New York. The Russians of all shades of political opinion were unanimous in their protest as soon as the matter became known after the arrival of the ship in New York, and the Bolshevist element, vigorously abetted by the other forces of unrest in the city, made a loud demand that the ship go direct to Petrograd. This outcry did not influence us at all, but the complete sincerity of the appeal from all the Russians for whom we were responsible was something which we could not disregard.

I may say that upon consulting Bakhmetff and other strong anti-Bolshevists here in America I was assured that the bitter sense of disillusionment on the part of the Russian people with reference to the French was so widespread in this country as to be practically unanimous. This feeling on the part of the Colony itself was the underlying basis first for our appeal and later for our own decision in the matter.

The determination to make the decision today was the result of a number of incidents, each one calculated to increase the unrest and excitement of the Colony and to make the question of the re-embarkation of its members upon the Yomei Maru without definite word in reply to the formal protests which had been made to us, a matter of increasing difficulty and danger.

It must always be remembered that the Red Cross has no legal control over the Colony and that if once its moral control were lost, it would be helpless in carrying out its original intention to restore the children to their parents and the adults to their homes.

The United States Government was in no position to help us, as the Colony was technically on the high seas, having never been formally admitted to the United States.

The incidents, which included the impossibility of distinguishing in the granting of passes between the bona-fide friends of the children and Soviet agitators, constant attempts of the children to escape from the confines of Fort Wadsworth, and finally a sad accident by which one of the children was accidentally killed by a guard, created an atmosphere which made the advancing of the decision in our judgment an absolute necessity.

It so happened that we had a meeting of the Executive Committee yesterday, and without asking them to give me instructions in the matter, I laid the case before them and I am confident that the step that I have taken meets with their approval.

Sincerely yours,
(Signed) F. P. Keppel
Vice-Chairman.

The *Yomei Maru* was scheduled to sail at noon, September 11. Captain Kayahara and his crew had been aboard for forty-eight hours to keep steam up so the cargo booms could be worked. On the tenth, a work detail of older boys had moved aboard to sort and distribute linen. At eight o'clock the morning of the eleventh, six Department of Justice agents came aboard and searched the ship for subversive literature. Burle Bramhall arrived at ten o'clock.

He was just about to mount the gangplank when three of the older boys began to descend it. Their faces were dark with anger.

"Where are you going?" Bramhall demanded.

"We're walking off the ship," one of the boys answered.

"Did you finish your work in the linen room?"

"No . . ."

"The children will be arriving in an hour. Let's get back to it."

"We're walking off the ship in protest," the boy said stubbornly.

"Oh?" Bramhall stood blocking the way.

This walk-off technique seemed contagious, first the P.O.W.'s, and now these boys. Bramhall did not ask their grievance, that could be negotiated later, the first thing was to reestablish discipline. For a long, silent moment the three husky Russian boys and the slender American faced each other.

"Okay, now," Bramhall said, "let's get back aboard." He

grasped the shoulder of the leader, turned him around and shoved him up the gangplank. The action was half good-humored roughhouse and half an ultimatum. Let the boy choose which. Under the momentum of the shove the boy stumbled up the gangplank a few steps, paused, then continued on up by his own volition. The other two boys trailed after him.

Once on deck Bramhall said crisply, "Now, what's the trouble?"

The boys pointed forward. There, from the open hatch of cargo hold No. 4 a column of smoke spiraled up. Thinking the ship might be on fire, Bramhall gave a shout and rushed forward to stare down into the hold. There were no flames, but a charred mass of smoking books.

"They burned our library," one of the boys said bitterly.

The library had been sent aboard by White Russians and had consisted of volumes of the classics, works of Tolstoy, Dostoevsky and Turgenev. Many of them had been beautifully bound in leather, some illustrated with steel engravings. They had been books cherished by their owners but unselfishly given to the children so they might become acquainted with some of their cultural heritage.

During their search of the ship for Red literature, the Justice Department agents had come upon these books in the hold. Not reading Russian, it was impossible for the agents to determine immediately if they contained subversive thoughts. As they leafed through the incomprehensible pages one can imagine the expressions on their faces—doubt, suspicion, frustration. The names of the authors should have vouched for the contents, but perhaps not. Perhaps in their minds the very language of Russia had assumed a subversive character. In any event, their duty seemed clear to them. If there was any doubt about these books (and in the absence of certainty there had to be doubt) they should be destroyed. They piled them together and set a match to them.

Books do not burn easily, especially good books that are well printed on fine paper and heavily bound. They tend to resist the flame, they smudge and they smoke, they make a dirty fire.

Bramhall looked down at the dirty fire and demanded of the boys, "Who did this?"

The boys shrugged. "Some men. They talked to the captain. He didn't stop them."

"I'll see what I can find out about it, but you boys get back to work in the linen room."

From the captain Bramhall learned that the book burners were Justice Department agents. The captain said that he did not believe he had the authority to stop them. He probably didn't. His authority was a thin and wavering thing under any circumstances.

Bramhall brooded until Riley Allen came aboard and then reported the story with some heat. "I think we should lodge a formal complaint with the Justice Department," he concluded.

"You do?" Allen said thoughtfully.

"What kind of example of American justice does this set for the children?"

"Not a happy one," Allen agreed.

"Besides, it's all so ridiculous. Suppose there *had* been subversive literature down in that hold—well, we're headed for Petrograd so what is the Department of Justice trying to do, keep Bolshevik propaganda away from the Reds?"

"If we make a formal protest," Allen said, "there will be an investigation. That would keep us here for probably another week." He gestured across the river toward the city. "We've had a good deal of trouble in New York and I think it would be well to get away. We'll sail on schedule."

At ten-thirty the children began to arrive, each one being checked off by number at the gangplank.

At eleven o'clock an ambulance pulled up beside the ship and out of it was lifted Maria Gorbochova. She was muffled to her chin in blankets, and her head was swathed in bandages, but her pale features held a happy grin. The doctors had operated successfully and she was going home with the rest of the children. As she was carried to the ship's infirmary, all the children shouted in happy surprise—their Maria was back with them! They took it as a good omen.

Bramhall, after checking the final child aboard, made a personnel report to Allen. Eight children and young nurses had been claimed by parents or close relatives in New York. One girl had died of meningitis. One boy had been killed. Two boys had sneaked off to New York for last-minute shopping and would miss the sailing. The Red Cross would eventually supply them with other transportation. With these exceptions, all the ship's company was aboard.

At noon the *Yomei Maru* backed away from her New Jersey pier and moved down the harbor. The children crowded the railings to look back at the diminishing skyline of the great city that had given them a mixture of memories.

TWENTY-THREE

As the *Yomei Maru* headed into the Atlantic there was an unaccountable gloom aboard ship. The Colony had won the dispute concerning France, each turn of the ship's propeller was taking them closer to home, the tumultuous days in New York had produced mutual declarations of love and trust between the children and the Americans, and still there was a heaviness of spirit.

Part of it was simply physical and emotional exhaustion. And part of it was the boredom of the sea. As the children stared over the side they saw waves that looked no different from the ones in the Pacific. It was as if nothing had changed, nothing really happened. For all their senses told them, they could be standing still, suspended forever in a grey and watery waste. They felt farther from their parents than ever. Home-sickness wrapped the ship in a muffled embrace.

Four days out of New York, Maria Gorbochova died.

As word raced through the ship, the children were stunned and disbelieving, as was the Red Cross staff. Florence Farmer, the chief nurse, had been almost constantly at Maria's bedside. For three days she seemed to be making slight but steady progress, and then on the fourth, at seven-thirty on the evening of September 15, she died.

Mother Campbell was supervising the final cleanup work in the galley when Riley Allen approached her and asked, "Mother, can you make a shroud?"

Her eyes widened with shock. "The little teacher . . . ?"

He nodded. "Just a few minutes ago. Can you make a shroud for burial at sea?"

"I can try," she said.

Life aboard ship must be practical, and so must death. At sea a shroud makes no effort to honor the body so recently and marvelously alive, its sole purpose is to dispose. It is simply a sack with weights.

Mother Campbell obtained canvas, a sail needle and twine, and two heavy iron bars. When she finished her work she took it to the infirmary and there the weights were inserted in the bottom of the sack, followed by the body of Maria Gorbochova. Finally, Mother Campbell sewed the sack closed at the top.

At dawn the next day the body was placed on a cot on the poop deck and there began the Russian Orthodox observance of death, twelve hours of vigil, songs and prayers. It was a poor catafalque for Maria Gorbochova, an iron cot and a shapeless sack, and all who beheld it were lacerated. The children had seen death before, ugly death, but never this.

This was like losing a member of the family, a loved older sister. There were no secrets withheld from Maria, because she could understand and, if necessary, forgive. She was their link between their own world and the world of adults, and she made the transition from one to the other less painful. But now she was gone, the link was broken. What they found hard to believe was not just the fact of death, but that Maria Gorbochova could be reduced to an ugly sack on an iron cot. There was a monstrous illogic, a cruelty they could not at first accept.

During the afternoon the ship's carpenter began building a wooden trestle and chute by the starboard rail. It was down this that the body would slide on its way to the sea. Each man and woman and child who heard the hammer blows felt as if his own scaffold were being erected.

Allen decreed that the actual burial should take place at ten o'clock the evening of September 16, after the smaller children had retired. At the appointed hour the older boys and girls, the teachers, the Americans, the prisoners of war, the Japanese crew gathered on deck. The shrouded body was placed on the wooden trestle. The boys' choir sang the final funeral hymn, their voices cracking with both emotion and adolescence. A prayer was said, the words accompanied by the low throb of the ship's engine and the swish of the propeller. The captain stepped forward to say a few words, unintelligible to all save the crew. Then at his signal the ship headed into the waves and the engine stilled and all was quiet.

Two crewmen grasped the trestle, tilting it up. The shroud moved, canvas rasping against the wooden planks. It gathered speed down the chute and fell clear in a moment of utter silence. Then a splash. A wreath of foam formed above the grave but then a wave erased it, leaving nothing to mark the spot.

On deck there was silence. It was the silence of grief beyond expression, the silence of the abyss observed.

The next day was bright with sun and shining sea. The burial had ended the darkness, had surfeited and then purged the spirits. Life aboard ship began to resume the normal rhythm. Dr. H. M. Coulter decided that the proper moment had arrived for the execution of his pet project. While in New York he had obtained the necessary materials to give the entire Colony intelligence tests. He planned to use the so-called "Terman Tests" which had been developed by the Army to determine the mental age or intelligence quotient in respect to normal averages. Coulter enlisted the aid of Dr. Davison and Dr. C. M. Gano in conducting and evaluating the tests. The children entered into them with enthusiasm, as if they were games.

After several days of interviews and paper work Coulter announced that he would like to report his results to the next staff meeting. Allen immediately convened a meeting to hear and honor Dr. Coulter's work. The report was an exhaustive one, but the end result was that the brightest child aboard ship was a thirteen-year-old boy named Boris Setkov.

"I propose that we have some little ceremony honoring him in front of the Colony," Dr. Coulter said. "Perhaps we can strike off a medal or a certificate for him. He should be the inspiration for the rest of the children."

Allen rubbed his chin. The name had a familiar ring but he couldn't quite place the boy. He said, "Maybe we should first interview him privately."

"Capital idea," exclaimed Coulter. "We can find out what his ambitions are for the future and perhaps have him prepare a little speech about them."

The boy was sent for and when he entered the cabin and looked about at the adults with complete composure, Allen remembered. This was the boy who had led the young band of thieves in pilfering the lifeboats shortly after sailing from Vladivostok.

Dr. Coulter did not know or did not remember, for he warmly shook the boy by the hand and informed him of his distinction. Then he said heartily, "Tell me, young man, what do you propose to become when you grow up?"

"I'm going to be a thief," the boy said.

Dr. Coulter blinked. The boy had obviously not understood his question. He repeated it. The boy again replied, "Yah boodoo vorom." (I am going to be a thief.) The interpreter assured Coulter that the translation was correct.

Dr. Coulter's mouth opened and closed a number of times without articulating any words. Finally he asked, "Why?"

The boy replied, "Things are very bad in my country and for a long time the only way to eat well and dress well will be to

steal. I shall study very carefully how to do it. I shall always
work alone, without any stupid assistants. I will be more intelligent than those who try to catch me, so I will not be caught.
For the next few years it will be the best profession to have."

There was a dazed expression on Dr. Coulter's face. He tried
to come up with something to counter the boy's cool logic but
seemed unable to gather his thoughts. Finally he waved his
hand in dismissal and Boris Setkov walked out of the room,
closing the door quietly behind him.

"He doesn't mean it," Coulter said to his associates.

"Oh, I think he does," Allen said drily. "He's been practicing
on our time."

The *Yomei Maru* was sailing through the Atlantic without a
destination. Each day Allen queried the radio operator for a
message that would assign them a Baltic port, but none came
through. There was good reason for this; the question which
Allen had thought settled was still being debated. A.R.C. European Commissioner Olds, under whose command Allen and
the Colony would soon pass, had not yet surrendered his point
of view.

The very day of Maria Gorbochova's funeral, Olds was writing a letter to American Red Cross Chairman Livingston Farrand in which he said:

Sending the Colony on to the Baltic States or to any point in
that region we feel is equivalent to losing control. We should
thereby be placing them in the area where they are fairly
certain to become a pawn in the political game. We have
talked this aspect of the case over within the past two or
three days with Colonel Ryan (Edward Ryan, American Red
Cross Baltic Commissioner) who very emphatically confirms
this view. He says no guaranty whatever can be given if the
Colony is landed in a Baltic port. There is no Government in
that part of the world which would not be embarrassed by a
demand from Moscow and there would be no way of resist-
ing very long wholesale repatriation, nor would it be pos-

sible to prevent all sorts of political propaganda from being spread in the Colony itself, consequently if the members of the Colony insist upon being sent on from France to a Baltic port we must contemplate relinquishment of Red Cross control and withdrawal of Red Cross protection . . .

Olds delayed the designation of a Baltic port until he could talk personally to Allen. He counted upon such a confrontation to swing policy back to his position. At noon Saturday, September 25, 1920, the *Yomei Maru* put in at Brest, France, where Commissioner Olds waited on the dock. He was immediately closeted with Allen.

Later, in typical understatement, Allen entered in the log for that day, "He (Olds) asked my opinion as to a possible review of the decision of not to remain temporarily in France."

In another log entry, some of the thrust of Olds' position was revealed. Allen wrote, "Colonel Olds went over in detail, and very forcefully, the present conditions in Petrograd and expressed also the belief that we would lose control of the Colony on arrival at a Baltic port . . ."

They were quite unlike, these adversaries in the tiny cabin aboard the *Yomei Maru,* and they *were* adversaries at this moment, however good their manners. Robert E. Olds was a massive man with a square, handsome face and a forthright, almost blunt manner. He had been a lawyer and he knew the skills of advocacy. He had the weight and the force to successfully administer and control the immense Red Cross relief program on a devastated continent. He was accustomed to the exercise of power.

Moreover, he had formidable arguments. He pointed out the fact that Finland, Estonia, Latvia and Lithuania had only the most precarious hold on nationhood. They had won independence from Russia at the time of the Revolution in 1917, not because the Kerensky government accorded it to them, but because it could not prevent their taking it. But now, in 1920, the Bolsheviks had consolidated their power and were openly

talking of retaking the Baltic States. Suppose they did invade
them at the moment the *Yomei Maru* sailed into port? Or even
if they didn't, suppose they demanded the immediate surrender of the Colony as the price of not invading? Could any of
the Baltic nations be expected to withstand such pressure?

All Olds was asking, he said, was that they play it safe, wait
and see what would happen, put the children in a French
camp until the political crisis was resolved. For two hours the
two men talked, and despite the pressure of Olds' facts and of
his considerable personal force, Allen held firm. He did not
deny the difficulties, he merely maintained that somehow they
could be overcome, that somehow the Red Cross must honor
its pledge to find the parents and reunite them with the children.

In the end Olds sighed and stood up and said, "The decision
has been made in Washington. Without your agreement I do
not feel I can properly reopen the question."

He did not have Allen's agreement.

Nine persons left the ship at Brest, parents or relatives having been found in France and England. Included were four
boys, Sergei and Andrei Fede, Constantin Frebulius and Andre
O'Connell; three nurses, M. Hiriokova, M. Malama, and Gir-
keria Kourgozova; an interpreter, Natalia Poloushkina; and an
educator, Zinaida Kamenetskaya.

On the morning of September 28, the *Yomei Maru* backed
off from her pier in Brest and turned her bow toward the
North Sea. Olds had promised to try to find a Baltic country
that would accept her, but there was no assurance. She sailed
on faith alone—Riley Allen's faith.

TWENTY-FOUR

The log for September 29, 1920, read: "About three o'clock in the morning our French pilot got off and an English pilot took his place. The Englishman will take us to the Kiel Canal, which he said is open . . . He told us that in addition to the dangerous waters and narrow channels through which we must pass, there are still many mines in the North Sea out of the Straits of Dover. These mines are being swept up as fast as found, but it will be years before the water can be assuredly free of them."

The *Yomei Maru* successfully avoided the mines and the shoals, and on October 2 Allen wrote in the log: "We were in the wide mouth of the Elbe River at dawn this morning, proceeding slowly upstream against a considerable current . . . Early in the morning we ran into the port of Cuxhaven and anchored just before eight o'clock off the quarantine dock. The German port quarantine officials came out in a small, rather shabby-looking tug, and the officials were shabby too. The red tape which I expected was not in evidence and aside from a few simple questions and a casual examination of the passenger list, there was little paper work done by the visitors. Dr.

Davison showed the chief doctor the hospital and this doctor looked at some of the children on deck, but no detailed physical examination was made on board, the German officials accepting the reports of our own doctors."

The passage through the Canal was uneventful except that it revealed the destitution of Germany. The log reported: "The stories of hard times in Germany and the German pictures of the future, painted by the visitors who came aboard, such as pilots, ships' agents and port officials, had a marked effect on the temper of our Austrian and Hungarian prisoners of war, inasmuch as they are soon to return to these conditions, or worse. They are now feeling anything but cheerful. Also the German papers which they receive give little grounds for optimism . . . There is no need for us to guard the gangplank at the Kiel Canal to prevent any of our people on the *Yomei Maru*—either Russians or prisoner employees—from going ashore. The German stories about conditions here were better than any number of guards."

The city of Kiel marked the eastern terminus of the canal. Beyond it lay the Baltic Sea, bordered on the south and east by Poland, still at war with Russia, and the Baltic States threatened by Russian invasion. Up to this moment the *Yomei Maru* had been in friendly waters. Ahead was uncertainty.

On October 2 Allen concluded the log with: "We lay at Kiel for one hour and a half, then headed out into the Baltic. No sooner had we moved from the dock than we began to feel the force of a wind sweeping in from the chill sea, and the first officer and a number of sailors were busy for hours lashing the two forward lifeboats . . . and making fast tarpaulins, hatch coverings and running gear. At four-thirty when I turned in, it looked as if we would be in a blow by morning."

Before retiring Allen sent the following wireless to Olds in Paris: "*Yomei* passed Kiel Canal October 2 all well stop have received no instructions yet stop if none received will proceed Helsingfors stop."

October 3 was Sunday, but it brought no rest to the *Yomei Maru*, for the wind had increased to gale force and the ship

Scrubbed, fed and clothed, the children prepare for the long box car trip to Vladivostok.

Halila, Finland—refuge after the tumultuous voyage aboard the *Yomei Maru*.

The bridge across Chornaya Rechka (Little Black River), scene of the final drama.

rolled and groaned in the towering waves. The storm-lashed decks were free of children; they were sick in their bunks below. Allen spent the day in the wireless shack trying desperately to get in touch with Helsingfors or Reval or any other Baltic port, but he had no success.

The following day saw the seas even higher and seasickness widespread. Allen sent a wireless message to several Baltic ports, hoping to reach Edward Ryan, A.R.C. Baltic Commissioner, in one of them. The message read: "Monday October fourth nine p.m. Yomei Maru about 400 miles from Reval stop having received no instructions expect to proceed Helsingfors which expect reach Wednesday night or Thursday morning stop if you have different instructions please wireless immediately stop all well aboard stop will be prepared quick debarkation stop"

The silence from both Ryan in the Baltic and Olds in Paris seemed unaccountable. With no direction from his superiors, Allen was on his own. He told Captain Kayahara to proceed to Helsingfors and he then dispatched the following wire on behalf of the Colony:

American Red Cross Reval stop Committee Children's Colony requests immediate delivery following telegram quote Gukovsky Centrosoyus Russian Cooperative Revel Estonia stop we request you inform Petrograd Parents' Committee that Children's Colony which left Petrograd May nineteen eighteen for western Siberia now under protection Amred Cross on way to Helsingfors on steam Yomei Maru signed United Committee Petrograd Children's Colony unquote ALLEN.

On October 5 Allen received the first word from his superiors. It was from Olds in Paris and the tone was peremptory: "Wire received stating you proceeding to Helsingfors stop your orders were report direct to Riga for further instructions stop we have not heard from Ryan designating Helsingfors but you understand you are to take final orders from Ryan."

Allen thereupon entered in the log the mild observation, "It is probable that Colonel Ryan has sent out instructions for me by wireless but they failed to reach the ship, although our operator has been constantly listening on the expectation of getting a message with information on which we could proceed."

The final entry in the log for the day read, "Late this evening we got Riga several times by wireless but there were no messages for the Yomei Maru to be had and no instructions forthcoming."

Dawn of October 6 came clear and crisp. The sea was fresh and sun-washed and when Helsingfors came into view it looked beautiful to the hundreds of eager eyes that ringed the rail. The entry to the harbor was through a narrow channel, buttressed on both sides by tremendous rock pillars which gave the impression of an ancient fortress gate. Once through the gate, the harbor was large and on this day full of ships of many flags.

The *Yomei Maru* dropped anchor two miles from shore at about ten o'clock. Customs men came out to the ship, but no public health doctors, for there was no official permission to land. Allen, Bramhall and the captain went ashore in a customs boat and when they climbed upon the large municipal dock they stood there for a moment and looked around. "I'd thought someone might be here to meet us," Allen said.

"One would have thought so," Bramhall said rather heavily.

"I'll telephone the American Consul," Allen said. "He may have some instructions for us."

He disappeared into a building and emerged a few minutes later with a wry smile on his face. "The consulate didn't know we were coming. I rather got the impression they had never even heard of us."

"Humph!" said Bramhall.

Captain Kayahara said nothing.

"I have the address of the Red Cross office," Allen continued. "We better go there and talk to Captain Elliott who is in charge."

When they got to the Red Cross office they found that Captain Elliott was having lunch at Hotel Kamp. Allen telephoned the hotel to page Captain Elliott and finally got him on the phone. He was having lunch with Captain F. D. Hopkins, senior Red Cross officer for Finland, who had come over from his headquarters in Vyborg to discuss the Children's Colony. They extended an invitation to join them for lunch.

"All week we've been trying to get a decision out of the government," Hopkins explained over the lunch table, "but they're terribly difficult to pin down. Feelings against the Russians run pretty high here in Finland."

"These are innocent children," Allen observed.

"You must remember that some innocent Finnish children have been killed by Russian bombardment."

"The healing must begin sometime."

"To be sure," Hopkins said with a touch of impatience, "but I am trying to explain the difficulties we face. Since the eighteenth century the Finnish people have been trying to throw off the Russian yoke. They finally won independence two years ago under the treaty of Brest-Litovsk. But what happens? While Lenin signed the treaty with one hand, with his other he sent arms to the Finnish Reds to subvert the new nation. During the civil war just ended an estimated fifteen thousand men, women and children were killed. To this day no final peace treaty has been signed with Russia. Depending upon what happens in the war between the Bolsheviks and Poland, Finland may be faced with another invasion. The moderate Republican Government, with whom we must deal, is little over a year old. It is opposed by the Finnish Right led by the war hero General Carl Mannerheim. Any appearance of being soft on Bolshevism would certainly bring this government down. And we are asking them to help return to Russia children who, it will be charged, may one day be enemy soldiers. To give the Colony asylum and assistance would certainly be hazardous for President Stahlberg's government."

Allen listened to the grim array of facts marshaled by Hopkins, then he said, "It has been my experience that men are capable of making hazardous decisions when their hearts are moved."

Hopkins said, "I am merely pointing out the fact that here in Finland the problems are formidable."

Allen smiled. "They have been formidable ever since we undertook the care of the children over two years ago."

Hopkins drained his coffee cup. "I understand that the Council of Ministers was considering our problem this morning. Shall we go to the Foreign Office and see what we can find out?"

They were received cordially at the Foreign Office but also in a manner that was apologetic, even shame-faced. After the amenities, they were informed that the Council of Ministers had refused them permission to land. The decision had been reached reluctantly, only after intransigent opposition by the Home Minister. By naming the Home Minister, the Foreign Office was giving oblique admission that it was fear of internal political consequences that had been the deciding factor against them.

When Allen returned to the ship he found everyone gathered at the rail eagerly awaiting his report. He pushed through the crowd with hardly a word and went directly to his cabin, leaving Bramhall the job of explaining what had happened. A pall fell on the ship, not only from the news but from the look of brooding pain that had been on Riley Allen's face. None of them could remember a time when he had not supplied the humor and optimism, the pure guts, but now he seemed drained of all resources. And so the ship became drained of all hope.

Alone in his cabin, Allen gave himself up to the darkest thoughts. If Finland, the largest, most stable and most prosperous of the Baltic States, dared not admit them there would be no hope of help from Estonia or Latvia or Lithuania. He had spent two years and sailed 14,600 miles to bring the children to what end? He tortured himself with statistics. The charter of the *Yomei Maru* was costing the Red Cross $4,500 a day, and this was aside from food and supplies and salaries,

aside from the $100,000 spent to convert the ship for their use,
plus the additional thousands that would be needed to recon-
vert it when returning it to the owners.

These costs became his personal burden and he felt all but
crushed. He wondered where he had gone wrong. He had had
a last chance to turn back, when in France Commissioner Olds
had pleaded with him to do so, but he had refused. Now he
wondered why. Was it stubbornness? Ambition? Or had it simply been the blind confidence of ignorance. If so, that was
culpable too.

There reached a point where the grueling self-examination
became self-abasement, and then self-pity. He brought himself
sharply out of this slough and said aloud to the empty cabin,
"All right, what's to be done?"

Turn as he might, he could find no alternative to Finland.
The other Baltic States were out of the question. Poland was
still at war with Russia. To try now to return the children to
France would bring them to open revolt. Somehow Finland's
Council of Ministers must be made to reverse themselves. This
seemed all but impossible of accomplishment, yet it remained
the only way to avoid disaster.

The next morning when Allen came on deck he was hollow-
eyed and sober-faced, but he was brisk. From that small sign
his associates took heart.

"The Home Minister is the key to our problem," Allen said
later that morning to Hopkins in the Red Cross office. "But for
his opposition, the ministers would have allowed us to land."

"So it seems," Hopkins agreed.

"Our problem is not so terribly large, then. We have only to
get one man to change his mind."

"Ah," Hopkins said ruefully, "I've had dealings with the
Home Minister and I'm afraid that any appeals. . . ."

"Who is close to the gentleman?" Allen asked, ignoring the
note of defeatism. "On a personal level. Who would be considered his close friend?"

Hopkins thought a moment. "There's a man named Jensen.
Extremely wealthy. A Finn who made his money in America

and has come back home here to retire. Quite influential in government circles."

"Perhaps he's our man."

"Mrs. Jensen and the Home Minister's wife are very close, I understand. They're both accomplished musicians and give afternoon musicales."

"*Mrs.* Jensen!" Allen said with sudden interest. "I think perhaps *she*'s our man!"

"Mrs. Jensen?" Hopkins asked.

"It just so happens," Allen said with a grin, "that the children are going to give a concert this afternoon and we'd all be very pleased if Mrs. Jensen would be our guest of honor."

Mrs. Jensen had never before attended just this kind of afternoon musicale and as she sat in a folding chair on deck she took in everything with eager interest. Fortunately, the orchestra had never played better and with less contention, and the girls' chorus had never sung with more angelic sweetness. Mrs. Jensen noted to herself how like Finnish children they all looked and she felt tears gathering. When Allen, sitting at her elbow, told her of their cruel separation from their parents and their wanderings over the entire globe, she unashamedly took out her handkerchief and blew her nose. When she finally left the ship at the end of the concert it was with firm step and a determined look in her eyes.

Late that afternoon Mr. Jensen telephoned to the Helsingfors office of the Red Cross and spoke to Hopkins. He wondered if the facts concerning the children aboard the *Yomei Maru* were as reported to him by his wife. He was assured that they were.

"Well," he said, "I guess we'll have to build a little fire under somebody."

The fire was both quick and effective. The very next day the Council of Ministers reopened the question of the children and voted unanimously to admit them to Finland. They also placed at their disposal, at no cost, a large sanitarium named Halila, now standing vacant.

TWENTY-FIVE

Halila had been built by Czar Nicholas II when Finland was a Russian province. It had been intended as a TB sanitarium for the exclusive use of the royal family, relatives and retainers, and was designed on a grand scale with an enormous main house and many outbuildings. The principal structure contained a central three-story rotunda, encircled by balconies from which opened almost a hundred rooms.

The Finns inherited Halila with their independence, and though they had not put it to use they had maintained its equipment in good order. Halila was ready to receive the children now on their way from Helsingfors.

The *Yomei Maru* left Helsingfors on October 10, sailed eastward through the Gulf of Finland and put in at the port of Koivisto where the children disembarked for the final time. Free of its long-held burden, the strangely silent ship headed for Copenhagen where, under the supervision of Clarence Rowland, she would be reconverted to her original purpose and returned to her owners. From there, too, the prisoners of war would be dispatched to Berlin, ending their long service to the American Red Cross.

A train ran part of the way from Koivisto to Halila, but the children had to walk the last eighteen kilometers. Their hearts quickened and they sang as they tramped through pine and birch forests and skirted the deep, clear lakes. Most of them had visited Finland when it was part of Russia, some had had summer *dachas* on these very lakes, and this march through crisp air was almost like coming home. But they were not home. When they reached Halila they were thirty miles from the Russian border, and it was to be a long thirty miles.

There were some good omens, however. Two days before their arrival at the sanitarium, Finland and Russia had signed a peace treaty. There would be no invasion, no capture of the Colony by Red troops. Some of the dire things predicted by Olds back in France would not come about. Riley Allen was having some luck. He needed some.

A.R.C. Commissioner to the Baltic Edward Ryan came to Halila to confer with Allen about the next steps to be taken. He looked rather like a matinee idol of the period, having blue eyes, a square and jutting jaw, and curls that marched across his head in tight and glistening rows. With his uniform he wore a winged collar and bow tie. Early in the war he had been A.R.C. Commissioner to Serbia and had been formally charged by subordinates with being "overbearing, intolerant and high-handed."

Ernest Bicknell, a distinguished A.R.C. professional, was sent to investigate these charges. In his detailed report he wrote, "Ryan lives a simple, abstemious life, clear, straight-forward—an open book. His devotion to the Red Cross, his earnestness, his industry, are beyond question . . . If an essentially difficult job is to be done requiring quick decision, prompt action, courage and iron resolution, Ryan is the man. These same invaluable qualifications may make a man at times seem arbitrary and inconsiderate."

This was the man who sat facing Riley Allen to discuss the next steps to be taken. He came directly to the point. "I believe it desirable that the children be repatriated with the greatest dispatch and your Petrograd Commission be dissolved."

He had reason for his blunt words. His Baltic Commission was feeding 22,000 destitute people daily, as well as giving a vast amount of supplies to deserving institutions. Now suddenly he had to pay for the Children's Colony maintenance out of his existing budget, a Colony he had not wanted sent to the Baltic in the first place. From his point of view this was certainly a situation calling for quick decision and prompt action.

"With all deliberate speed," Allen agreed.

Ryan seemed to walk around the word "deliberate." Finally he said, "When will you be prepared to send the children to the border?"

"As soon as we hear from their parents," Allen said. "We have some Estonian children whose parents are presumably in Estonia, some Latvian children and, of course, Polish children. I do not propose to send any child into Petrograd until we have a letter from a parent telling us to do so."

"That may pose some difficulties," Ryan said.

Allen agreed.

"You are aware there is no communication between Finland and Russia? There's a peace treaty but no diplomatic relations."

"I understand that Estonia has diplomatic relations," Allen countered. "I have had printed up the names and last known addresses of all the children now here at Halila. I suggest that we enlist the aid of the Estonians in getting this list sent to the Parents Committee in Petrograd, along with the request that the parents write to their children, stating their desires about their placement."

"And if we are unable to contact the parents?"

"Then we could not, in good conscience, send the children across the border."

"And in that event, what would you propose to do?" Ryan asked stiffly.

Allen replied, "I would propose that we do not allow that to occur."

Ryan departed with the promise to seek Estonian aid in establishing contact with the Russians. Within ten days the Russian government responded, but not in the manner the Red Cross had hoped. The Finnish government received a cable from Moscow signed, "Tchicherine, Commissar of The People to the Foreign Affairs." The message read:

I am informed that a Japaneses [sic] ship having on board 725 children Russian taken out of Russia against their own will and against the desire of their parents by the American Red Cross which has the intention to send to the Russian border of Finland only a part of these children and a few educators declaring that they can not be sent before their parents will be located in this country. The Soviet Government is fully compettant [sic] in the cares due to children of Russian citisens [sic] and throws off with indignation the idea that the American Red Cross could have something to do with the location of the parents in Russia which even could not be done by the American Red Cross. We request to quarter the children immediately and to send them as soon as possible to the border of Russia where they will be received by the Committee representing their parties [sic]. These children being on the territory of Findland [sic] I request you to proceed with their delivery and their transportation.

Ryan and Olds had predicted just such pressure by the Soviets, and had also predicted the inability of any Baltic country to withstand the pressure. They had underestimated the Finns, however. These doughty people made one reply to the Red commissar; they announced merely that they were forwarding his cable to Allen. That was the last word they said on the matter, to Russia, to Allen, to anyone. Allen ignored the cable and continued his effort to establish direct contact with the parents.

Autumn is short in Finland and by October the long winter began to settle over the countryside. Classes were resumed and life was not unlike what it had been in Vladivostok, except here there was an air of expectancy. Each day might bring the magical news that they were to travel the last thirty miles and be home. Under such conditions who could really concentrate on grammar or algebra? And too, there were many exciting and secret projects afoot—the children were making farewell presents to give to their American friends.

The girls had asked for yarn and knitting needles, the boys were spending long hours in the workshop; all this in the most conspiratorial manner. Scarves, mittens, socks, ashtrays, tie racks were taking shape and each night were hidden under cots until they would be presented on that glorious, but sad day of farewell.

That the day might never arrive was a possibility kept from the children. The lines of communication had been set up as far as the Americans were capable of setting them. The Soviets had been informed that all correspondence from Petrograd should be sent to the Estonian government in Tallinn; from there it would be sent to Ryan's A.R.C. headquarters in Riga, Latvia; then to Hopkins' A.R.C. office in Vyborg, Finland. Vyborg was sixty kilometers from Halila and it was visited twice weekly by Allen or one of his staff. They traveled by drosky until the snows, then by sleigh. Each trip supplied them with instructions from Ryan and money for operation of the Colony and mail from back home in America. But nothing from Petrograd.

The last week in October Hal Davison made the trip to Vyborg. The assignment was partly to give him relief from his obstreperous charges. After sitting on the animal spirits, the resentments and the adventurism of twenty teen-age boys, a sixty-kilometer trip in zero weather was no hardship at all.

Late in the afternoon, just as twilight sent long purple shadows over the snow, a steaming horse pulling a sleigh trotted into the grounds of Halila. On the sleigh was Hal Davison returning from Vyborg. The sleigh stopped in front of the main building and Davison crawled out from under the mountain of furs and went directly to Allen's office.

"Riley, there was mail for us at Vyborg."

"From the States?" Allen asked.

Davison's elaborate casualness broke. He took Allen's arm and pulled him to the front window and pointed to a mound of sacks that filled the sleigh. In almost a whisper he said, "From Petrograd!"

Contact! Direct contact with the parents at last!

The two men turned and shook hands with each other, grins on their faces. Then Allen sobered. "Get the sacks in here without drawing any attention. We'll have to read those letters before they're passed on to the children. If they contain bad news . . ." he shrugged, "somehow we'll have to cushion the shock."

They did not contain bad news. Only one parent, out of the hundreds who wrote from Petrograd in this and later batches of mail, requested that his child be sent elsewhere than home. Nor did a careful reading of the letters reveal any government censorship. Here was free and unobstructed communication. The Red Cross terms had been met.

After supper that evening the entire Colony was assembled in the rotunda of the main building. All sorts of rumors had been flying around and no one knew exactly what to expect. As Allen stepped before the children, they quieted immediately and were half-hopeful, half-fearful.

He smiled and said, "You have received letters from your parents." A gasp went through the rotunda, all at the same instant, as if from a single throat. Allen continued quickly, "Not all of you have letters, only about two hundred. But more will be coming later. If your name isn't called tonight, you'll probably get a letter next week."

Allen reached into the sack just behind him, looked at the name on the letter and called out, "Ekaterina Zubkova."

A seventeen-year-old girl rushed forward, grabbed the letter

and went off into a corner to read it alone. She read only the
first two words, "Darling daughter, " and burst into tears.

"Tatiana Pozner," called Allen.

"Sergei Lepuhin."

"Vladimir Kazakoff."

"Alexandre Filipova."

"Eugen Dimitrieff."

One by one they ran forward and then darted off to distant
corners to devour the letters alone, like famished animals
guarding a morsel of food. Few could read more than the first
words without weeping. Soon all the letters had been passed
out and the tears of the fortunate ones were matched by those
who had not received a letter. The rotunda was full of muffled
sobs—joy and grief sounding the same.

Final plans now began rapidly to take shape. Communication was established, not only with the parents in Petrograd,
but with the Soviet government in Moscow, and it was arranged that the first delivery of 132 children would be made
across the Russian-Finnish border on November 10. Subsequent deliveries would be made about ten days apart as
parental approval was received.

There was a farewell party at Halila on the evening of
November 9. The balconies were decorated with freshly cut
evergreen boughs, there was a great bowl filled with fruit punch,
and trays loaded with cupcakes frosted pink and white. Out
from their hiding places came all the presents and soon the
Americans were loaded down with caps and mufflers and mittens. The Russian teachers didn't give presents to the Americans, but something infinitely more precious—letters of thanks.
The one given to Mother Campbell and signed by all the
teaching staff read:

Dear Mrs. Campbell: Telling you good-bye we want to
express you how much we all teachers and educators regret
that your activity in the Colony has to come to an end. We
want to tell you how much we appreciate your love for the

children, your kindness to everybody, and how thankfull we
are for all your work and all your cares, this won't be ever
forgotten by the children or anybody of us. Believe us all
respecting you and thankfull.

It was a gay party until bedtime when those children scheduled to depart the next day suddenly realized this would be
about the last time they would see the Americans. As they
clustered around them to express their thanks and say good-
bye, many of them burst into tears.

"We don't want to go," they stammered. "We want to stay
with you."

What they meant was that they wanted to go but also to
stay, they wanted things to change but to remain the same.
During the most turbulent and dangerous time of their lives
these Americans had been their only source of comfort and
safety and discipline, and they couldn't stand the thought of
just turning their backs and walking away. They wanted their
real parents, but they didn't want to lose their substitute parents in the process.

The Americans were caught up in the same wrenching emotion, for they loved these children as their own. Each Red
Cross man and woman held the conviction that the days and
months spent with this Colony would forever be the most important and rewarding of his entire life, and they were all
reluctant to put an end to them. They, no less than the children, shrank from this final moment.

There were a dozen children clustered around Riley Allen
when he looked down and saw eight-year-old Anna Amelina.
She was a shy, fawn-like child and her eyes held such suffering
that he could not resist bending down and kissing her on the
forehead. She immediately began to cry. He picked her up and
her arms went around his neck in a desperate grip and her
grief became uncontrolled. He took her off in a corner away
from the rest of the children and held her on his lap until her
sobbing ended. It took a long time, but finally she was quiet,

except for quaking gasps for breath. He began talking, telling
her how lonesome her mother and father had been for her and
how happy they would be to have her home. This brought a
fresh burst of tears. At last, when this had passed, she confided
a secret to him. She told it in a whisper, for it was heavy with
shame.

"I can't remember," she sobbed. "I can't remember what my
mother looks like."

Allen held her away from him and looked into her eyes and
said, "You don't have to remember now, Anna. Because you'll
remember tomorrow."

"I will?" she asked uncertainly.

"You will," he said with conviction. "When you get to the
railway station in Petrograd there will be a big crowd of
people but you'll recognize your mother. No one in the world
looks exactly like your mother, and you'll know her when you
see her."

For a long moment she pondered this information. She did
not understand how it could be, yet she had never known this
man to say anything but the truth. She looked up to search his
face and found it grave. Suddenly it smiled at her and through
the tears the smile was wiggly and watery but it was familiar
and vastly reassuring. All the alarm and the shame drained out
of her and she smiled wetly back.

TWENTY-SIX

The Chornaya Rechka (Little Black River) marked the border between Finland and Soviet Russia. It wandered down out of the snow-swept hills to empty into the Gulf of Finland, a nondescript river so small as to be on few maps except those of the immediate region. There were scars here of the recent fighting. A water tower, its tank pierced by an artillery shell, stood high and dry, and a heavy timbered bridge had been destroyed and lay half-submerged in the river.

Reconstruction had begun in a small way; a footbridge had been built from bank to bank. It was a poor thing, as rickety as the peace it seemed to symbolize, but men could walk across it. And children could walk across it on their way home.

At nine o'clock on the morning of November 10, there was a flurry of activity on the northern shore of the Chornaya Rechka. There came into view a caravan of sleds piled high with luggage and paper-wrapped parcels. All this was unloaded and stacked near the bridge. The sled drivers clustered together to talk in low tones and look across the river to the south where they saw nothing. An hour passed, and a column of marching children came into view. There were 138 of them and they were accompanied by a dozen adults, including several Finnish soldiers. The subdued children went to the pile of luggage where each found his own and stood beside it. They looked across the river but saw nothing.

Another hour passed. And then another. The Estonian government, intermediary in all the arrangements, had said the transfer would take place at ten o'clock. Was there a last-minute breakdown of some sort?

Shortly after twelve noon there was a shout from one of the older boys and he pointed excitedly across the river. Men were coming from the south. They wore ankle-length greatcoats and peaked cloth caps embroidered with the star of the Red Army. They were a platoon and they carried no visible arms.

The Russians came to the bank of the river and conferred together. One of them started out on the footbridge, stopping midway where a pole and a white flag marked the exact center, the border between the nations. Riley Allen, accompanied by an interpreter and a Finnish officer, started out from his side. The Russian stood with feet braced against the swing of the footbridge, hands behind his back, and on his square young face he had placed an expression of stern aloofness.

Allen stuck out his hand and the Russian seemed disconcerted, unsure of what the new revolutionary mores called for in such a situation. Finally he took the proffered hand and shook it briefly. He identified himself as Commissar I. Subotin and said that he was authorized by the Commissariat of Education to receive the children.

Allen took off his mittens and from an inside pocket produced a sheaf of papers. "I have one hundred and thirty-eight children and seven adults, all with relatives or parents in Petrograd who desire their return."

Commissar Subotin said, "You are instructed to deliver to us all Lithuanian, Latvian and Estonian children. They are legally citizens of the Russian Socialist Federal Soviet Republic."

At this very moment back in Halila the Lithuanian, Latvian and Estonian children were being prepared for the trip back to their newly liberated homelands. There could be no retreat on this issue; the Red Cross could not send them to Petrograd. Would the entire transfer fall apart now at this late moment on the issue of the Baltic children? Allen looked at Subotin to measure him.

He was young and self-conscious, unaccustomed to power and therefore uncertain of its limits. He was likely to take extreme positions if his dignity seemed threatened. If Allen met him head on by rejecting his demand, Subotin would have to react and at the very least stalk off the bridge without accepting the children waiting on the Finnish shore with such solemn and hopeful eyes.

Allen said, "Commissar, I am not authorized to discuss the Baltic question."

Subotin considered the reply. If the American had no authority, well, that was that. It was beneath the dignity of a Soviet Commissar to discuss such important problems with a nobody. This would be taken up later, on higher levels.

With a wave of his hand he said, "I will accept the children you have here."

Allen noted with relief the patronizing tone in the Commissar's voice. He said, "I have here the names, addresses and medical records of each child. Also, any indicated continued medical treatment. I'll call them by name and we can process each child."

"Nyet . . . nyet!" exclaimed the commissar. "I have other important work to do and I cannot stand here on this bridge all day." He reached for the papers in Allen's hand. "I will take your word about the records. Just send the children across."

"Commissar Subotin," said Allen, retaining his papers, "I shall require from you a signed receipt for the children. It would be well for both of us if the count was absolutely correct. Each child has a number and I suggest that he call it out as he crosses over and together we check it off the list."

"As you wish," the commissar said.

Allen signaled toward the shore and the children began a

single file parade across the bridge. As they came to the middle of the swaying span they announced their numbers and looked up at Allen for the last time. They were so full of a mixture of emotions that they could only murmur a last "thank you" and hurry on.

There came Tatjana Nikolenko and she was still holding the hand of her little brother Gregorii who had grown a foot taller during the two years of Red Cross care. Behind them was Peter Azaroff, the boy who had refused a safe winter with the Siberian farmer so that he might return with food to the starving Colony. There was Natasha Lebedeva, walking with rounded shoulders and wan face. She was the child who had been handled by the Japanese sailor and would bear the scars forever. Leonty Diebner came with firm step. He was eighteen now, had grown to manhood with the Americans. He was the boy who had spoken out in defense of the Red Cross at Madison Square Garden. There came Ilin Kartasheff, the boy who had wrestled with the Japanese aboard the *Yomei Maru* and unwittingly started all the trouble. Toward the end of the line there came Boris Setkov, the boy who was going to be a thief. His thin, intelligent face was impassive, but alert for new opportunities.

Allen saw paraded before his eyes an accounting of the Red Cross guardianship, the successes and the failures. He tried to draw a balance, but he need not have. The overwhelming success was that these children had been plucked from the midst of slaughter, they had been saved, they were alive, they were going home.

Gradually the Finnish shore emptied and the Russian shore filled. Finally the children were once more together, standing on their native soil for the first time in many long and fearsome months. Their excited voices rose in the still air, and into a landscape that was dead and cold they brought life.

They began marching south, singing as they went. Allen, standing alone on the bridge, hoped they would look back. But they did not. And soon they were gone.

At last Allen's responsibility was ended, but he was surprised to discover that he felt not relief but loss. For an irrational moment he almost wished they could have all stayed together in Halila, but he was immediately ashamed of the thought, for it was a selfish one. No, he had done the right thing by uniting the children with their parents, but he realized now that this did not mean he would be free of them. For the rest of his life he would feel concern for these children, he would constantly speculate on what they might be doing. Their lives would hold pain and joy, despair and hope, for that was the destiny of all men, but he hoped the good would overbalance the bad, and he hoped they would remember the time they had had together.

At last he turned away from the vast and empty landscape and walked slowly back to Finland, the bridge swaying beneath his feet as he went.

Epilogue

The scene on the shores of the Little Black River was repeated eight times until, on January 26, 1921, the last child was delivered home and the American Red Cross Siberian Commission was liquidated. Riley Allen's final official act was to forward to Washington a meticulous accounting of each child who had been under his care for over two years:

Children sent to Estonia:	October 25	4	
	November 22	8	
	December 29	3	
	January 4	3	18
Children sent to Latvia:	October 26	9	
	December 7	3	12
Children sent to Finland:	November 30	1	
	January 16	1	2
Children sent to Germany:	January 25	3	3
Children sent to France:	September 26	2	
	January 25	1	3
Children sent to London:	September 26	1	1

| Children sent to Tomsk: | January 26 ...... | 1 | 1 |
| Children sent to New York: | September 10 .... | 3 | 3 |

TOTAL DELIVERED TO RELATIVES OUTSIDE OF PETROGRAD 43

Children sent to Petrograd:	November 10	138
	November 18	59
	November 29	221
	December 4	64
	December 13	96
	December 20	67
	January 4	40
	January 13	5
	January 26 (final) .	45

735

Forward 778
Casualties 2

TOTAL 780

Number of children originally sailing from Vladivostok
on July 13, 1920 780

With the liquidation of the A.R.C. Siberian Commission, the
volunteer personnel returned to their regular occupations. Drs.
Eversole, Davison, Coulter and Gano entered private practice
in various parts of the United States. Ward Walker returned to
his home in Maui, Hawaii, to manage a great sugarcane plan-
tation. Mother Campbell settled down with her family in
Woodland, California. Burle Bramhall entered the brokerage
business in Seattle. And Riley Allen returned to Honolulu and
resumed his job as editor of the *Star-Bulletin*.

During the following years Allen became one of the Island's
outstanding civic leaders. He was, successively, president of
the Honolulu Chamber of Commerce, president of the Advertising Club, vice-president of the Foreign Trade Council
chairman of the Institute of Pacific Relations, chairman of the
Hawaii Chapter of the National Foundation for Infantile
Paralysis, recipient of the Veterans of Foreign Wars' Citizen-

ship Medal, and received academic honors from the University
of Missouri and the University of Washington. He was a leader
in Hawaii's long fight for statehood. In 1960, he finally retired
as editor and general manager of the *Star-Bulletin* and became
a trustee of the Farrington Foundation, a fund left by his
former boss, Wallace Farrington. Today, at eighty-two years of
age, he appears daily in his office in Honolulu's Stangenwald
Building where he has become an elder statesman consulted
by all the island's political, civic and ethnic leaders.

Looking back over a long and honored life, Riley Allen sees
his Red Cross service and the saving of the Petrograd children
as his single most important accomplishment. During four
decades it has remained a living thing with him, for he is in
constant correspondence with many of the children, not only
in Petrograd (which became Leningrad) but in the various
European countries to which many of them emigrated.

Allen had hardly returned home when the children began to
send him letters detailing the events of their lives. On March 8,
1921, Olga Timofeieva wrote:

. . . For the present am not working anywhere, only studying English with Anna Alexandrovna Zakovoy. She resides at
Zavodsky and I walk there daily to her for my lessons. Of all
our Colonists there are only three left at the Zagorodny Community: I, Shura Burmistrova and Julia Turunen. Valia Pav-
olva, Marusia Isakova, Assia Zueva, Niura Kovaleva and Katia
Kerbunova were sent to the Internate where they will study
. . . Vera Muravieva of the Kurgan Colony got married and
lives very good . . . I would like to know something about
you and your assistants. How nice it would be to meet you
again to be able to express you our ardent thanks for all you
have done for us. We realize only now how much trouble we
have done to you while living at the Red Cross . . .

Many of the parents also sent their thanks and to them Allen
wrote:

The American personnel with the Children's Colony has
regretted very much that events make it impossible to meet

the parents of the children who have been so long in our care. We have received many of your letters of thanks and we are happy in knowing that your children are once again with you and that you will find them healthy, well fed and in condition to proceed with their education and with the responsibilities that will come upon them as citizens of Russia.

It is also our hope that at some future time we may meet you, the parents of these children, and tell you that if it has been a happiness for you to receive them, it has been as great a satisfaction for us to have been able to fulfill our trust undertaken when we first saw these homeless children in the perilous situation of western Siberia two years ago.

The sincere greetings and good wishes of the Red Cross are herewith sent to the parents of the children who have been in our care.

Riley H. Allen
Chief Executive, Petrograd
Children's Colony.

Some of the younger children did not get around to writing Allen for a number of years. In December 1926, Assia Fisser wrote:

Russia
Leningrad
Zahorodne, House 6, Apt. 1

Dear Mr. Allen:

I risk writing to you although I am nearly sure that you have forgotten me. And no wonder if you have, for it is six years since we parted and the little girl of twelve when you used to play with has become a young girl of eighteen.

I want to tell you that I shall never forget your great kindness to me during our trip through Siberia, Japan and America to Finland. The memory of those happy days is very dear to me. I wanted to tell you so ages ago but couldn't write not knowing the language. Now that I am learning English I seize the first opportunity for writing to you. Better late than never, isn't it?

As you are sure to have forgotten my face, I shall send you my photo next time, just to show you what I look like now. I had the bad luck to lose all my American snapshots on the way home.

How are you getting on? Don't you intend to come over here?

We shall be delighted to help you in any way we can. Hoping to get an answer soon, I remain with best Christmas greetings,

Your little friend of former days,
Assia Fisser.

There was also correspondence between Allen and the former prisoners of war. Typical was a letter from Eugene P. Hetenji, living at Vienna, VII. Kaiserstrasse 83, c/o Argentor-Werke, Austria:

I am in receipt of your kind Christmas card and the reminiscence of the past affected me so deeply that I weeped for joy and emotion . . . I remember very often the time passed with the A.R.C. and I am pleased that I had the honour to be in your care; this was a pleasant time for all persons being in the service of the A.R.C., this important charitable institution of the States and the biggest benevolent society of the world. The Russian "Djetskaja Kolonia" and we all, former prisoners of war, we are all indebted to the A.R.C. and especially to you, Colonel Allen, for all your kind heartedness and for all the good works you made for us in generally and for me especially.

This unique correspondence continued over the years, surviving the wars and passions that convulsed the world. And whatever the propaganda against America, the members of the Petrograd Children's Colony (now in late middle age) have known the truth.

Riley Allen and the other Red Cross volunteers have been for them the symbol of America. Remembered are the ways in which they dealt briskly with catastrophe; how they took off their jackets to wash the filthy, disease-ridden body of the stranger; bound up the horrible wounds of the mangled soldier; fed the bloated, unlovely starving. These Americans were convinced, despite the contrary evidence that almost daily assaulted their senses, that mankind is worthy.

And believing it can make it so.

⑦ Irkutsk
Sept. 8, 1919

⑧ Vladivostok
Sept. 19, 1919

⑨ Muroran,
Japan
July 15, 1920

⑩ San Francisco
Aug. 1, 1920

ROUTE OF THE
**Wild Children
of the Urals**